Allosaurus

Ankylosaurus

Brachiosaurus

coelophysis

Diplodocus

Hadrosaur

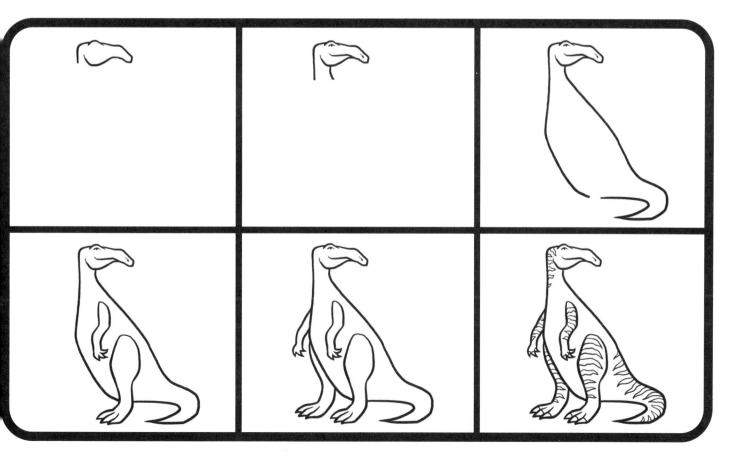

Iguanodon

Megalosaurus

Pachycephalosaurus

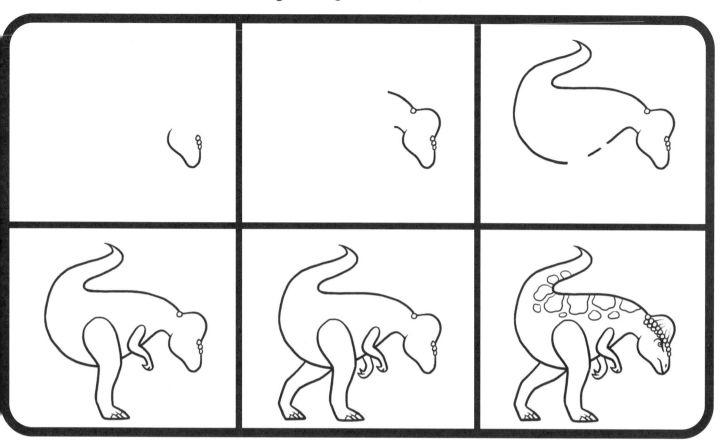

Parasaurolophus

Plesiosaurus

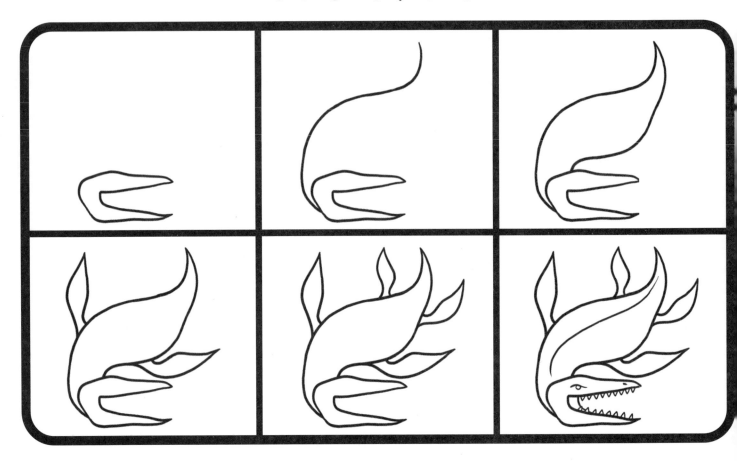

Pliosaurus

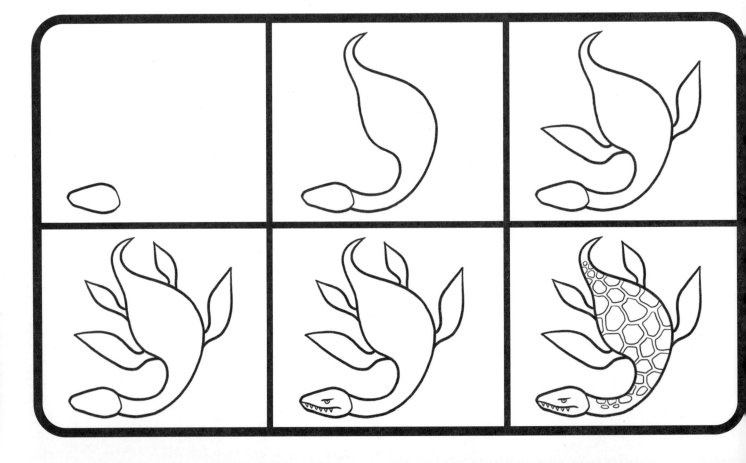

Pterosaur

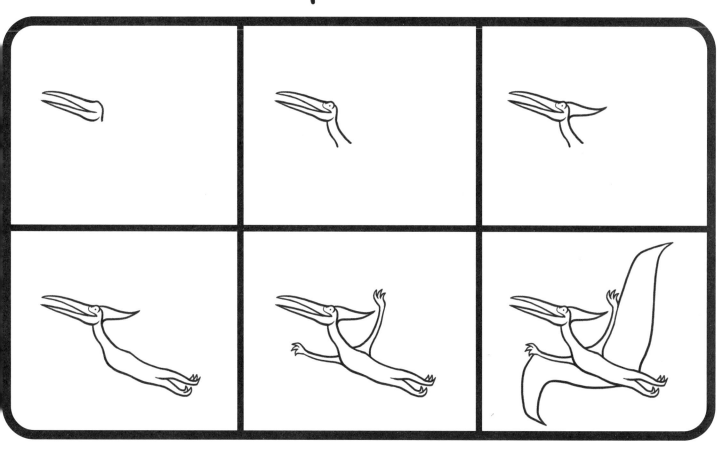

Spinosaurus

Stegosaurus

T-rex

Triceratops

Velociraptor

Cannon

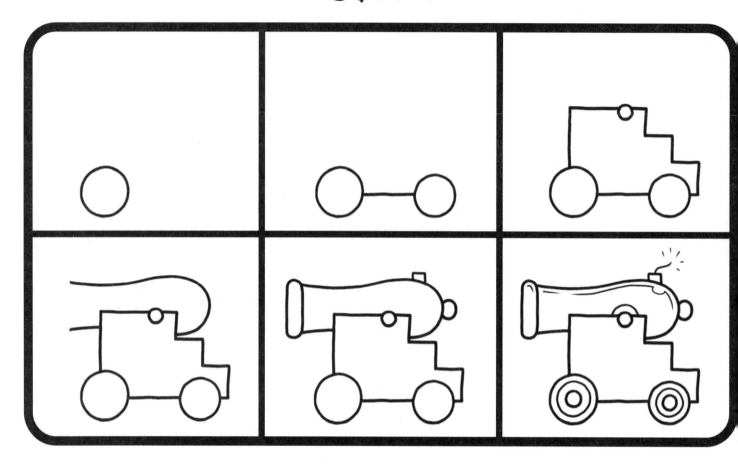

Jolly Roger

Parrot

Treasure Chest

Pirate Ship

Captain Blood

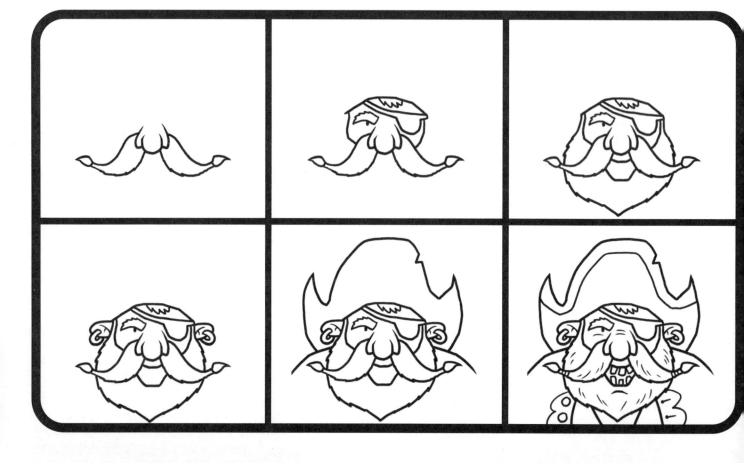

Scarface

Little Jack

Peg-Leg Pete

Sea Shanty Sam

Lookout Larry

Jake the Cabin Boy

Salty Sid

Lazy Liam

foredeck fred

cannonball callum

Dolphin Fish

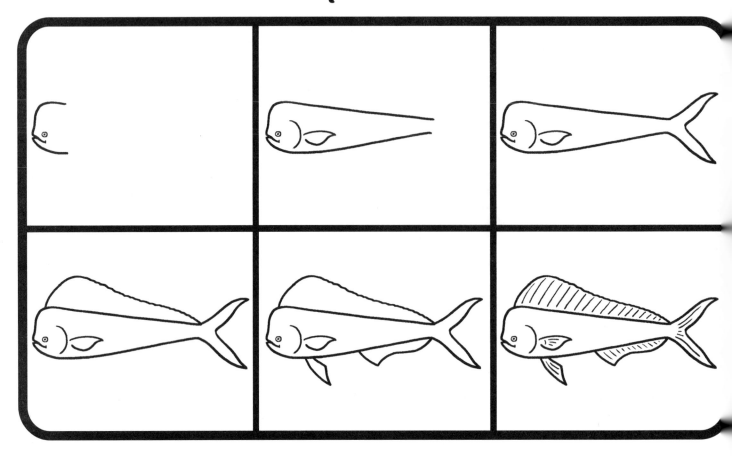

Yellowfin Tuna

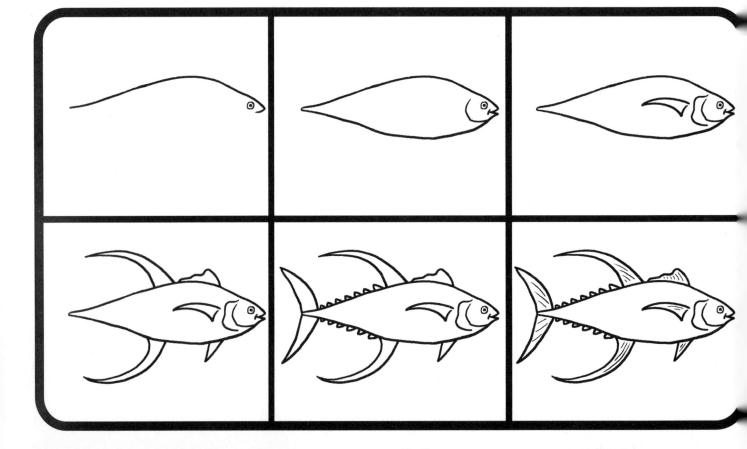

Rockhopper Penguin

Northern Right Whale

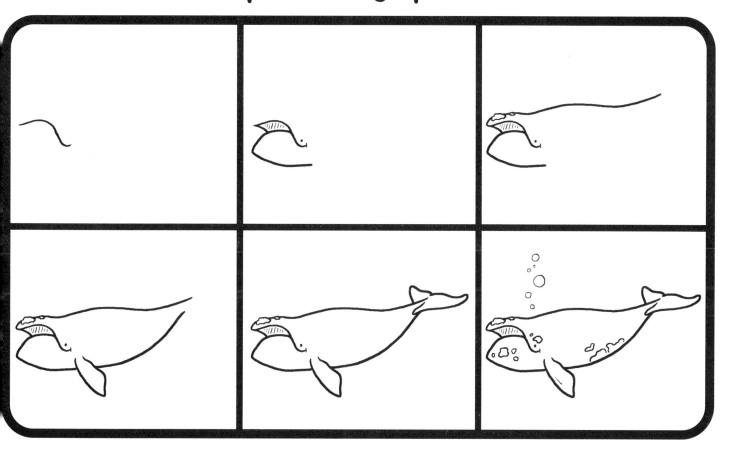

American Train

Spy Plane

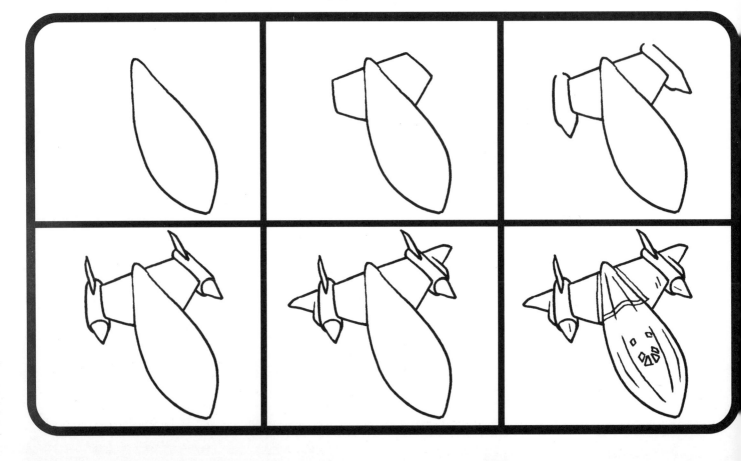

formula 1 Racing car

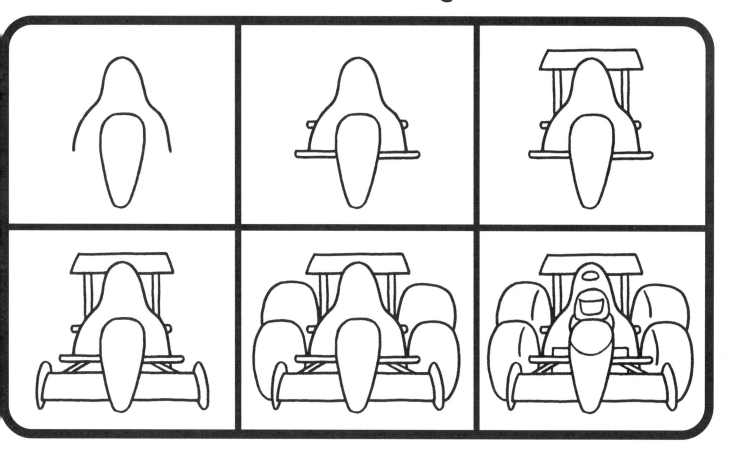

Road Roller

Rocker

cool Man

Leader

Cool Dude

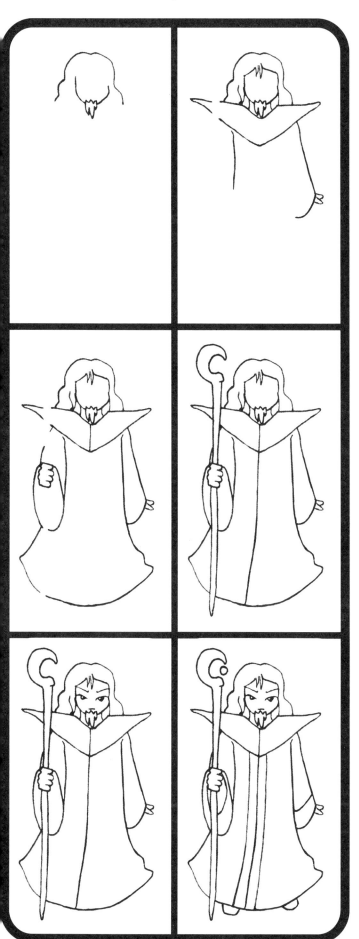
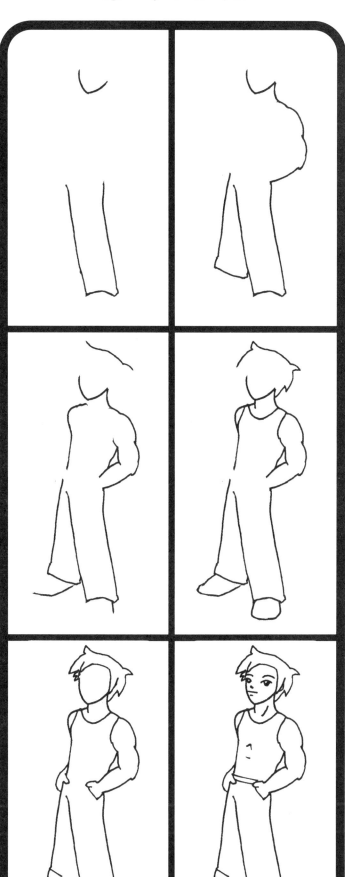

Banded Pipefish

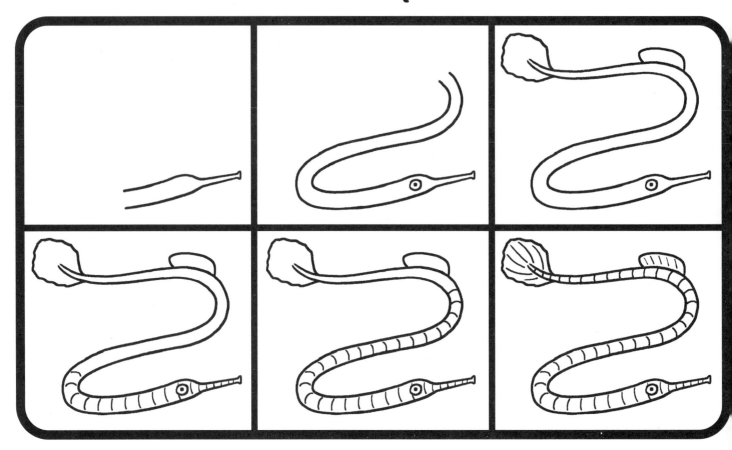

Puffer Fish

Shrimp

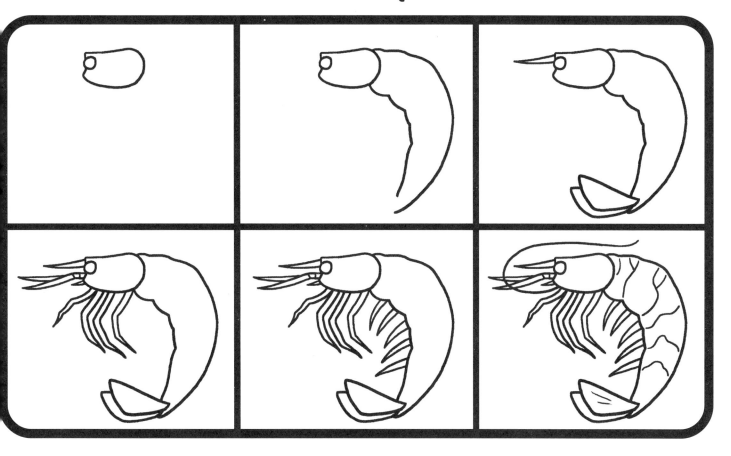

Dugong

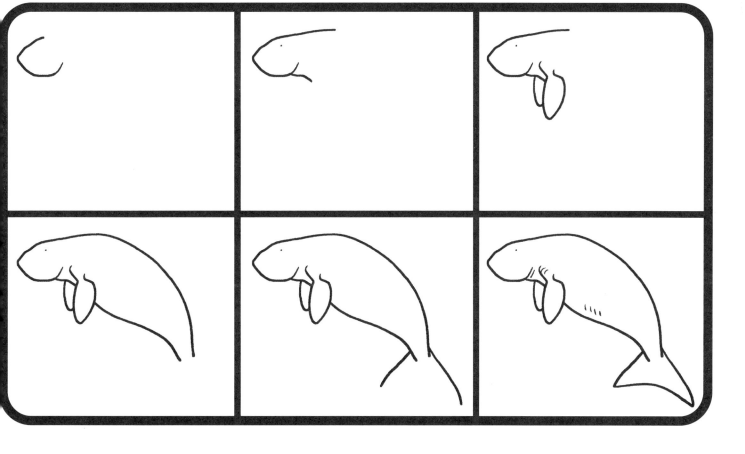

Cruise Ship

Chopper Bike

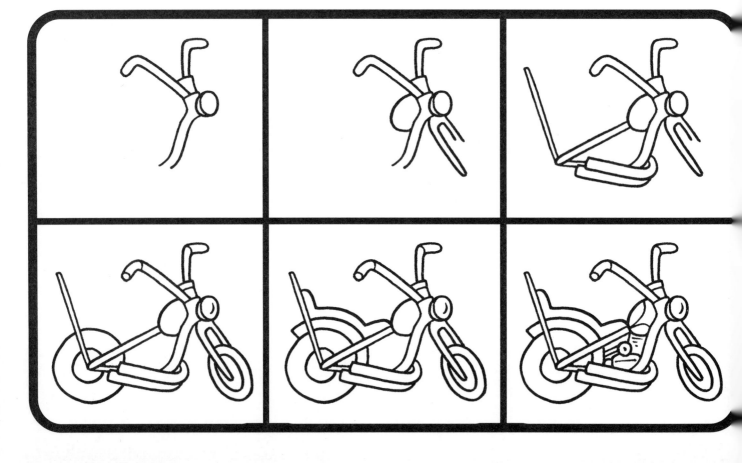

747 Jumbo Jet

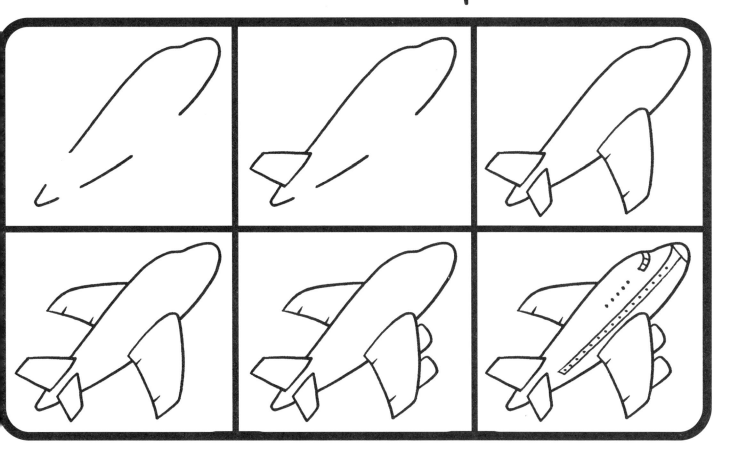

Custom Car

Robot 1

Robot 2

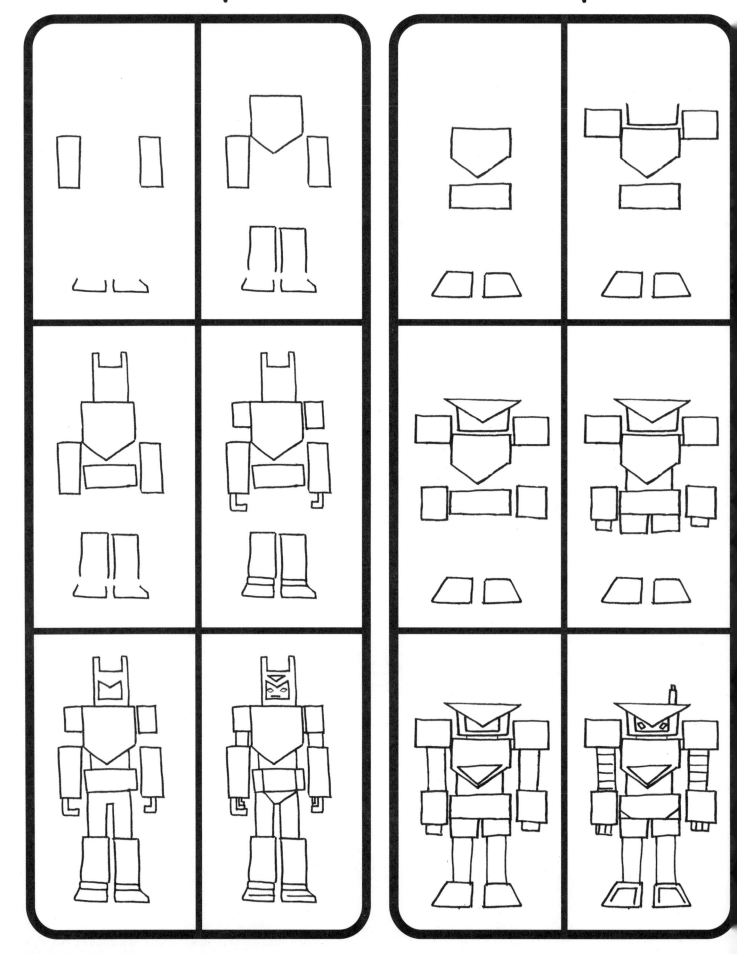

Robot 3

Robot 4

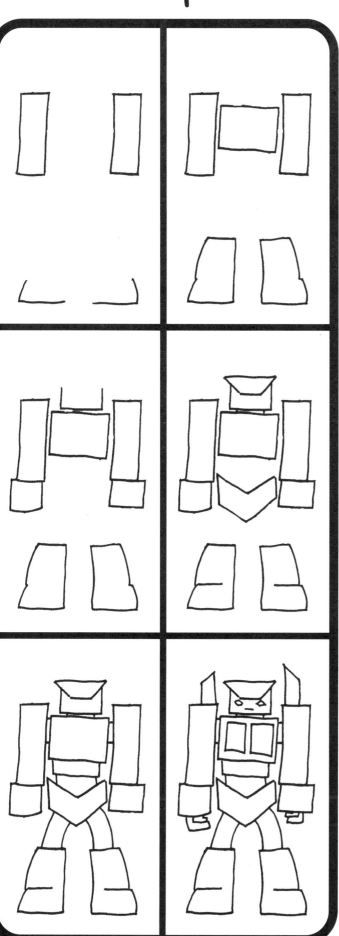

Parrot fish

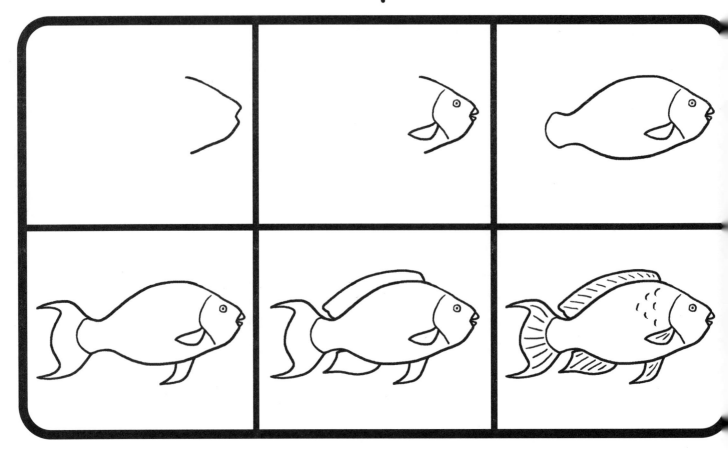

Chinstrap Penguin

Lionfish

Bonnethead Shark

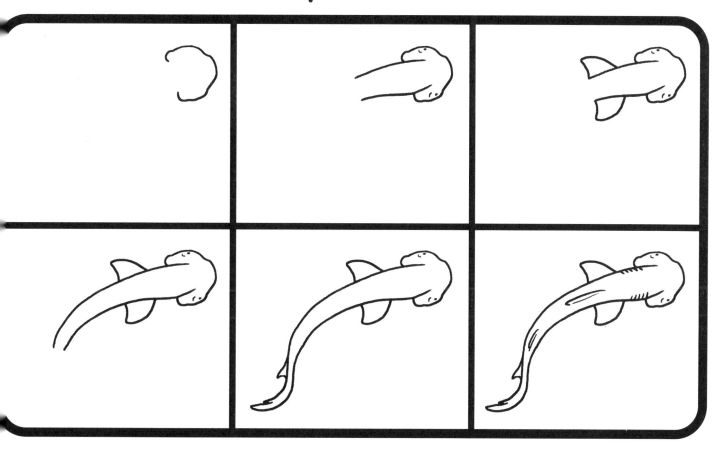

Jeep

Bullet Train

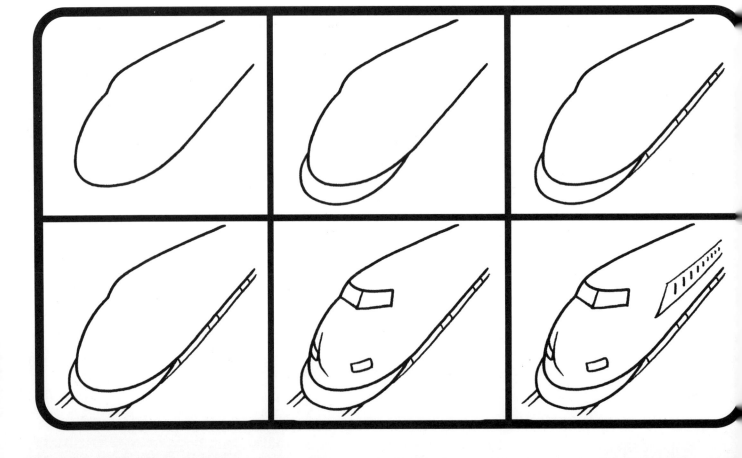

Motocross Bike

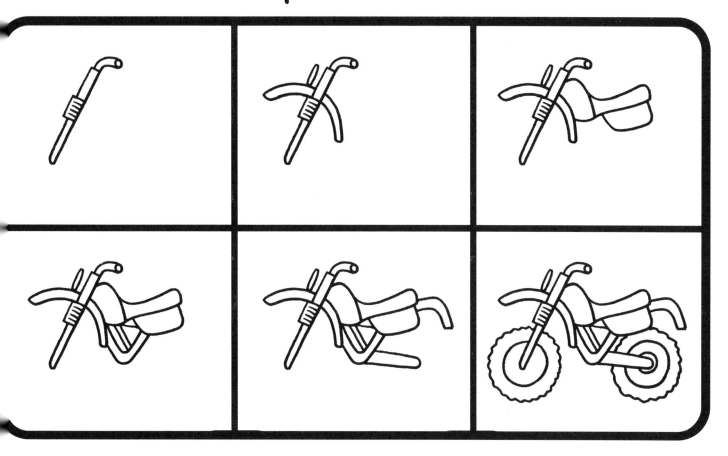

Traction Engine

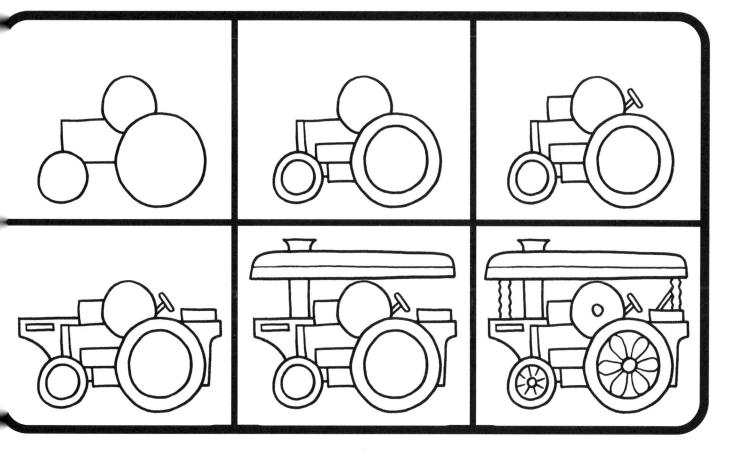

Robot 5

Robot 6

Robot 7

Robot 8

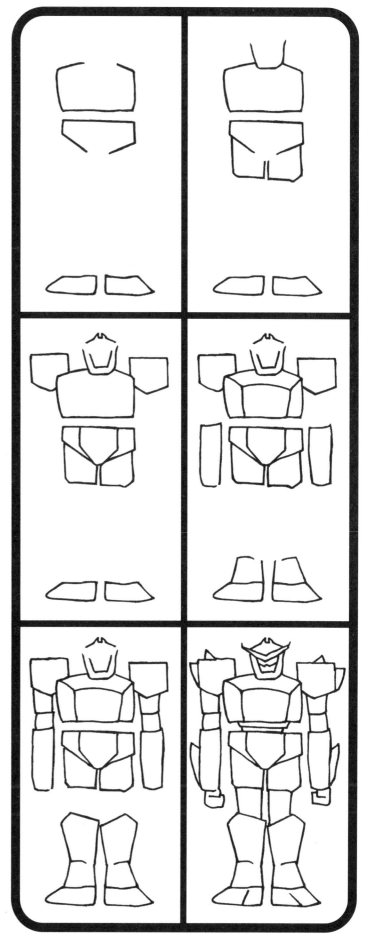

cuttlefish

Pilot whale

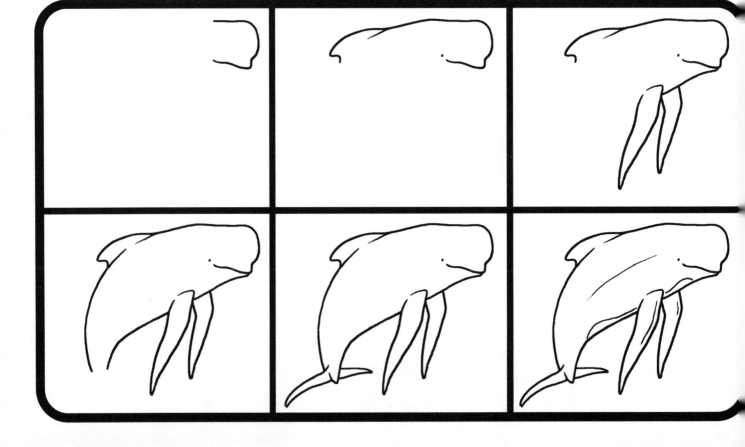

Skate

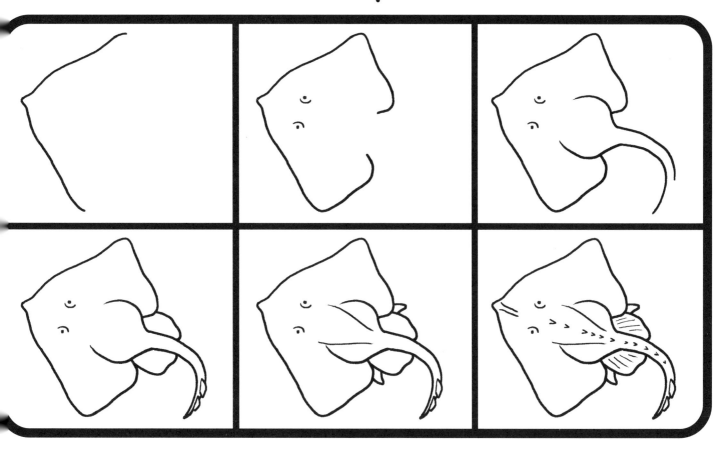

Hermit crab

Stealth fighter

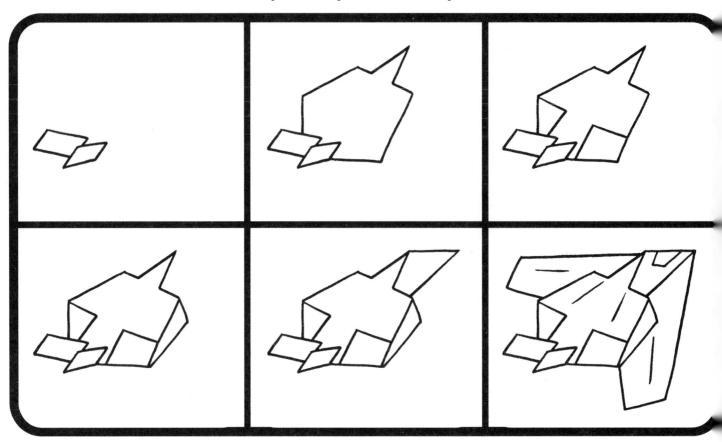

The first car

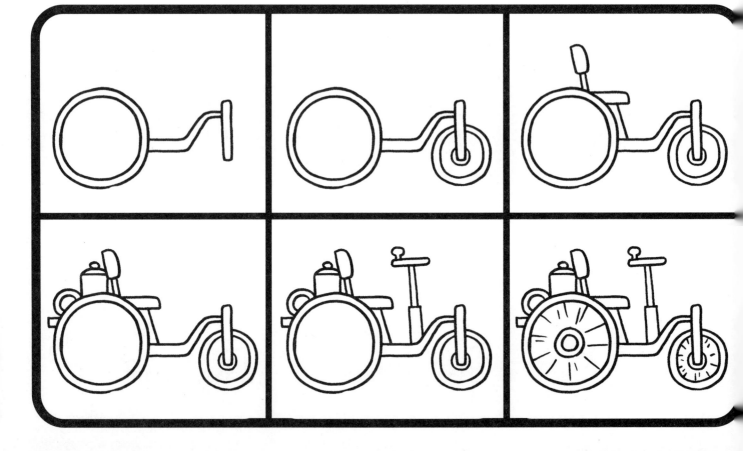

Dumper

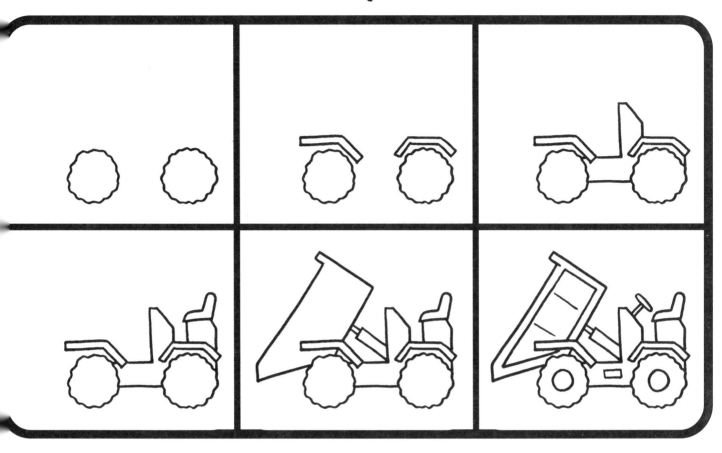

Cadillac

Anglerfish

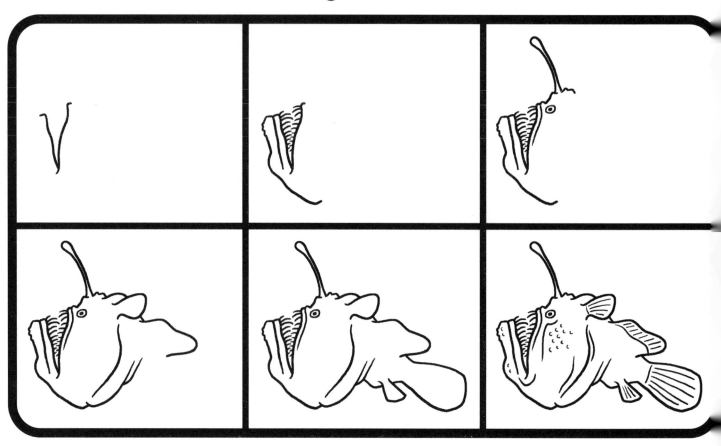

Marine Iguana

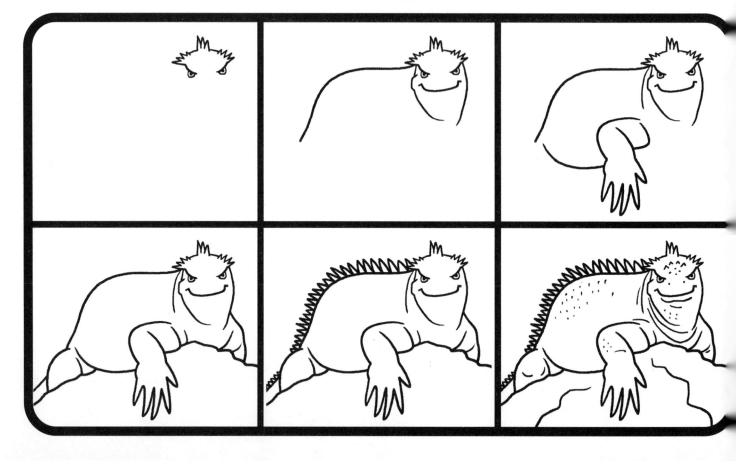

Humpback Whale

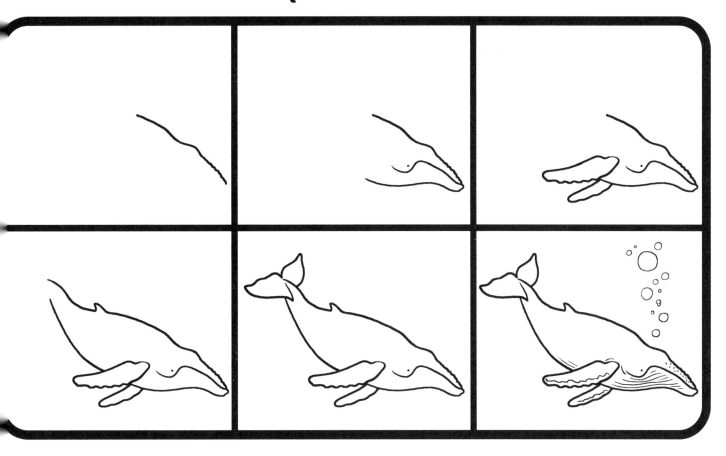

Flying Fish

Shy Boy

Bandana

Hoody

Ready to Go

Sea Slug

Sea otter

Horseshoe crab

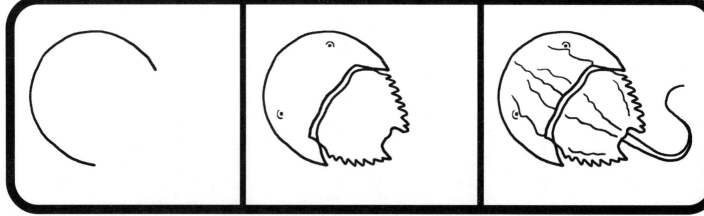

Clown Knife Fish

Moon Jellyfish

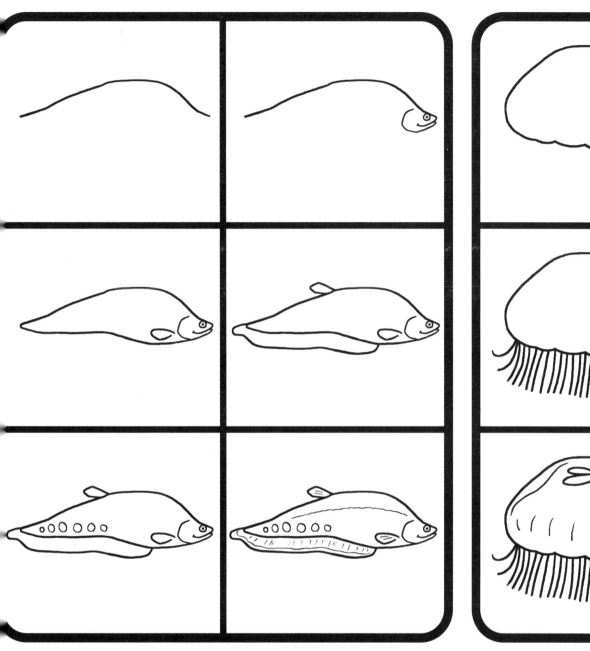

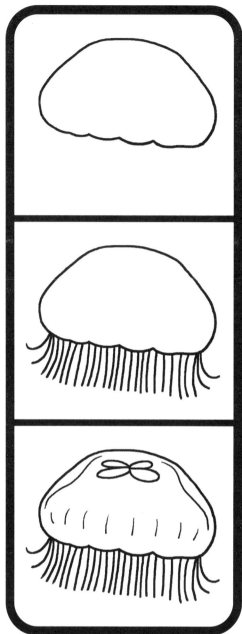

Big-Eye Thresher Shark

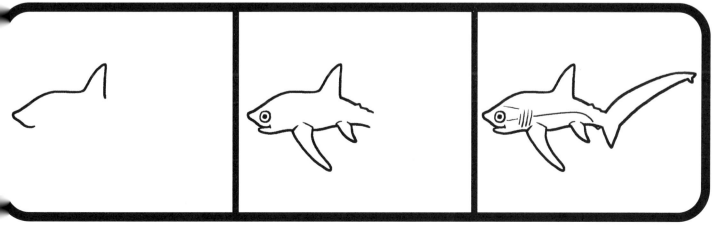

VW Beetle

Transit Van

Hang-glider

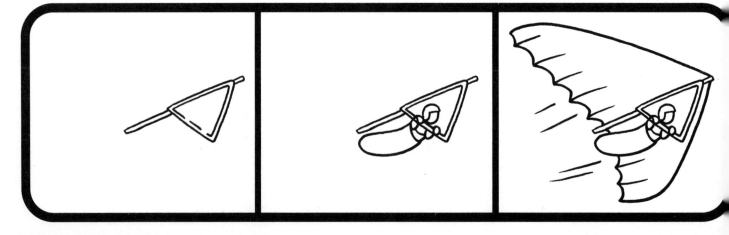

funicular

Rocket

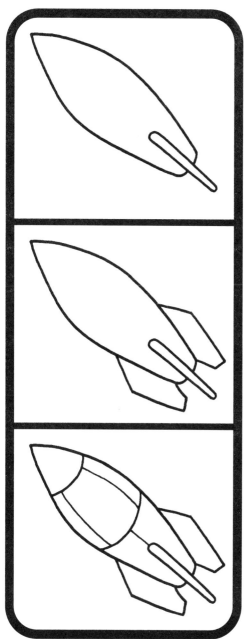

Lindbergh's 'Spirit of St. Louis'

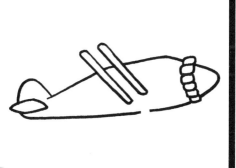

Fed Up

Demure

Thinking

Snozz

Gargoyle

Snorky

Gumph

Jarred

crab

Nessie

Matilda

Eyeball

Sloppy

Trog   Hairy

Slither

Hag

Bull

Snout

Rough

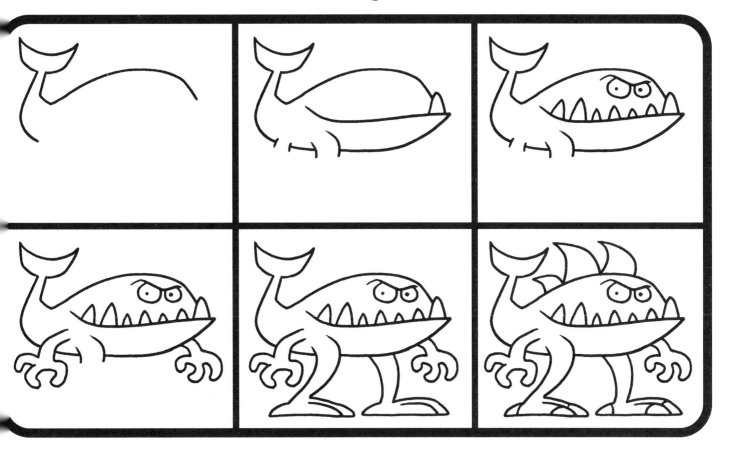

Troll-In-The-Box

Batty

Snurkle

Mertle

Spider

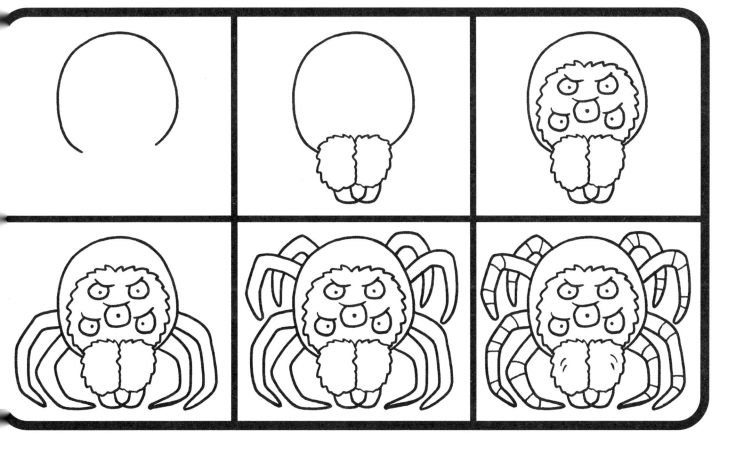

Shaggy

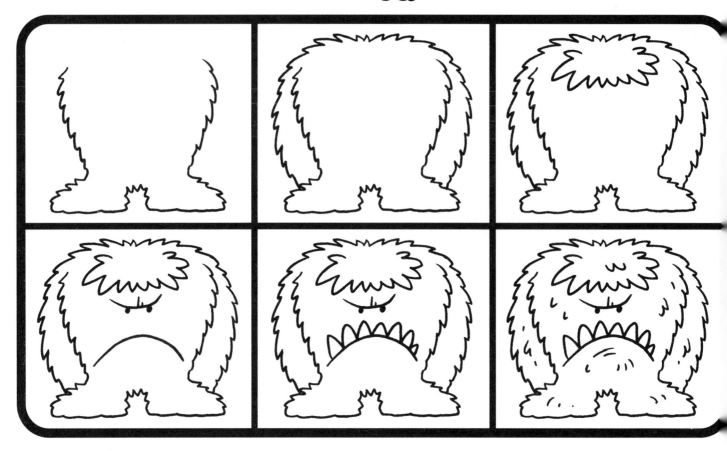

Wavy

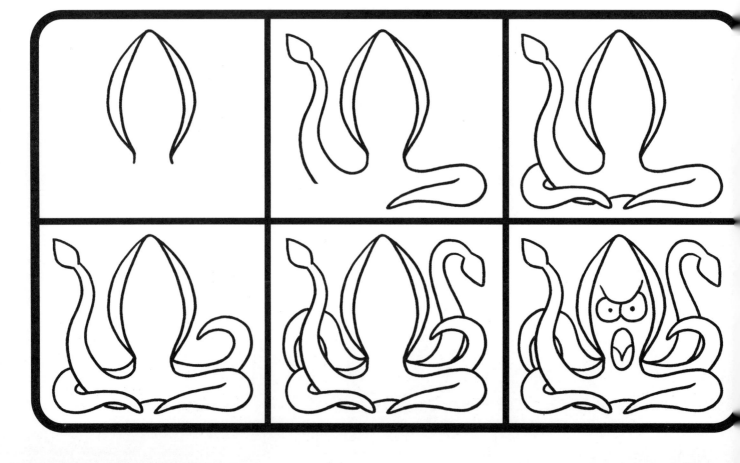

Pet

Vampire

Rah

Blob

Dev

Rock

Slimey

Slug

Flokk

Gumble

Warty

Dragon

Ted

Smelly

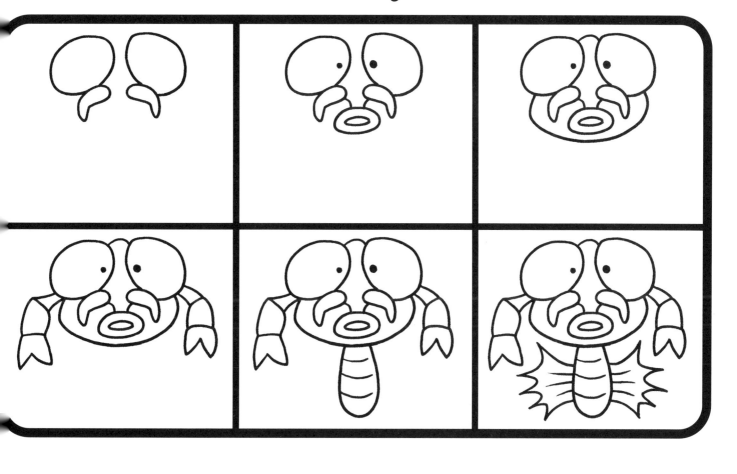

colly

cloaked

Sharky

Larry

Potty

Verm

Horn

Tree

Stocky

Mummy

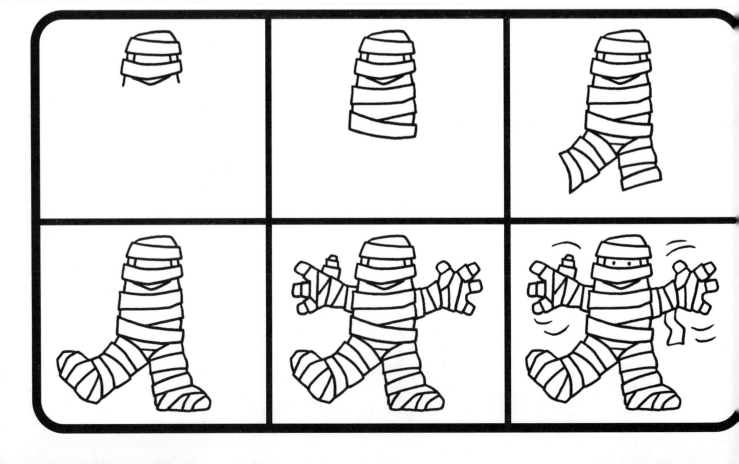

Big one

Bendy

Eavesdrop

Squabble

Skull

Snail

Rambo

Gloom

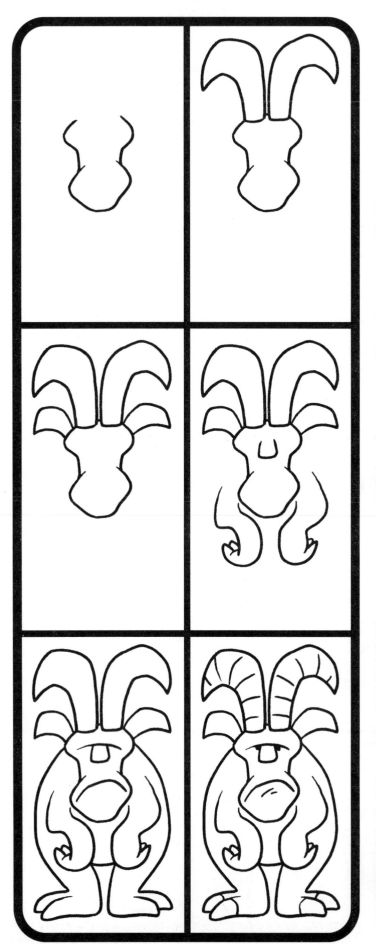
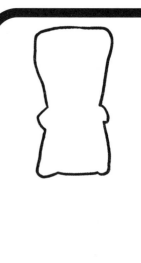

cyclops

Glum

Scary

Medusa

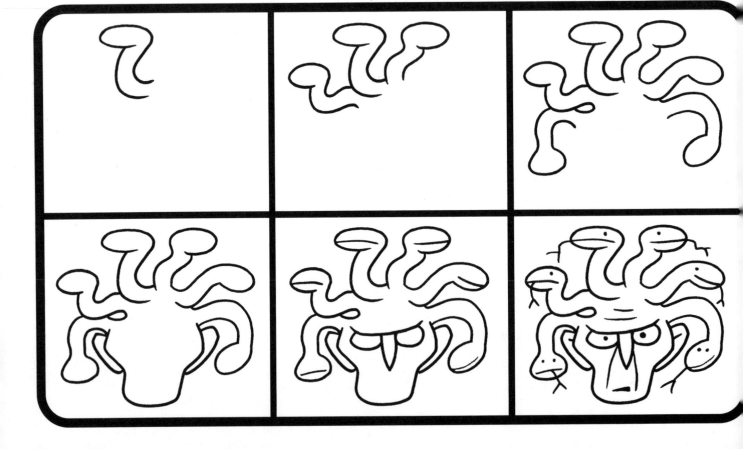

Jagged

Aaargh!

Troll

Bert

Hal

Nerd

Phantom

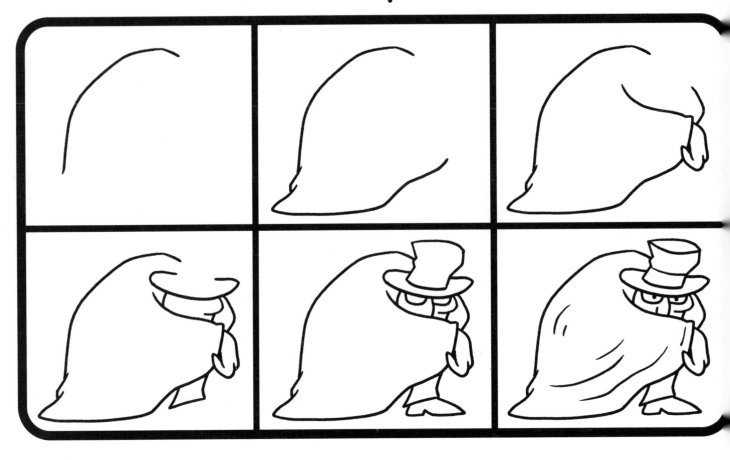

Squat

werewolf

Robot

Lippy

Merlin

Granny   Grandad

fingers

Pumpkin

Spot

Triton

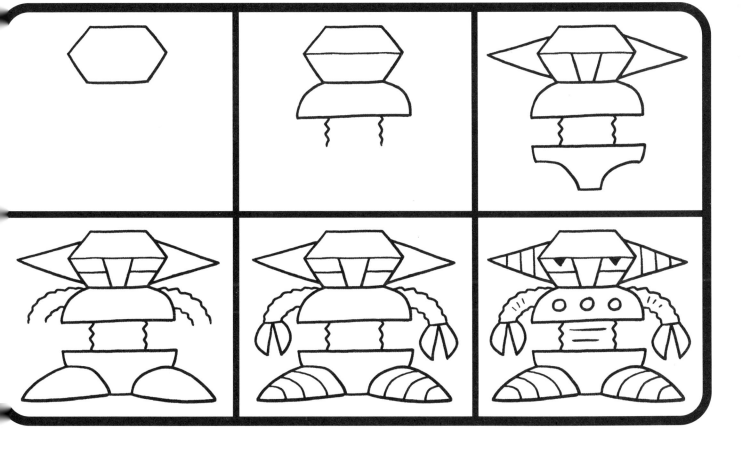

Baby

Happy

Growl

Wingding

Google

Johnny

Exterminate

Vanilla

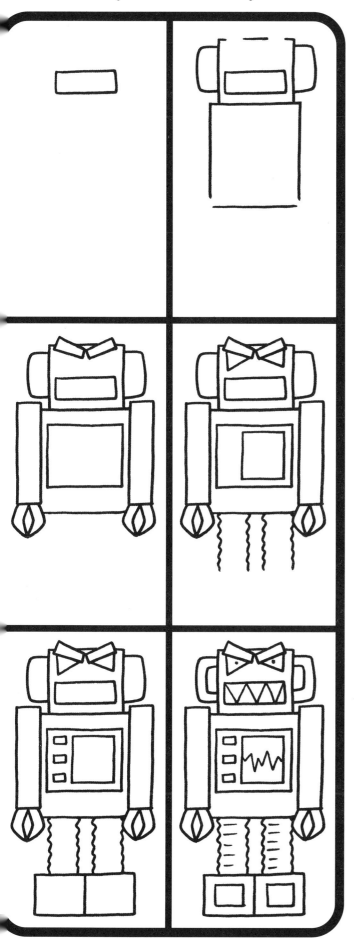

Hattie

Bulldog

Venus flytrap

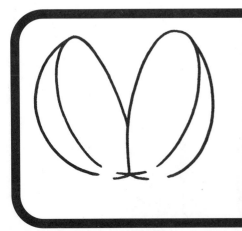  

Slurp

Horned Beast

Big Mouth

Snorkel

Helmet

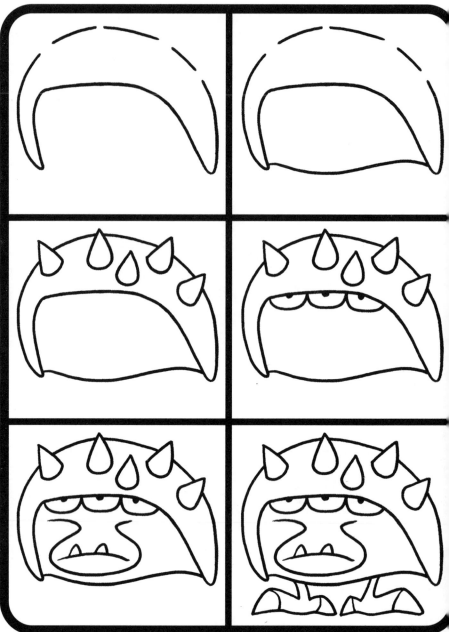

Herm

Beaky

Woo

Slump

Goggle Eyes

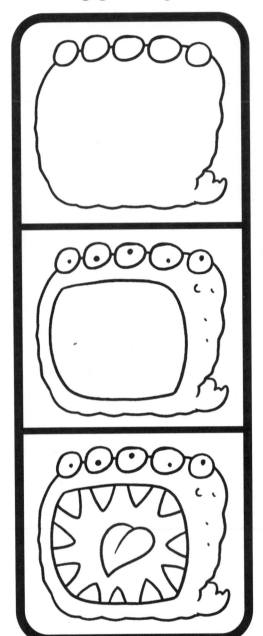

Truck

Slime

Fairy

Wizard

Minotaur

House Goblin

Ice Queen

Yeti

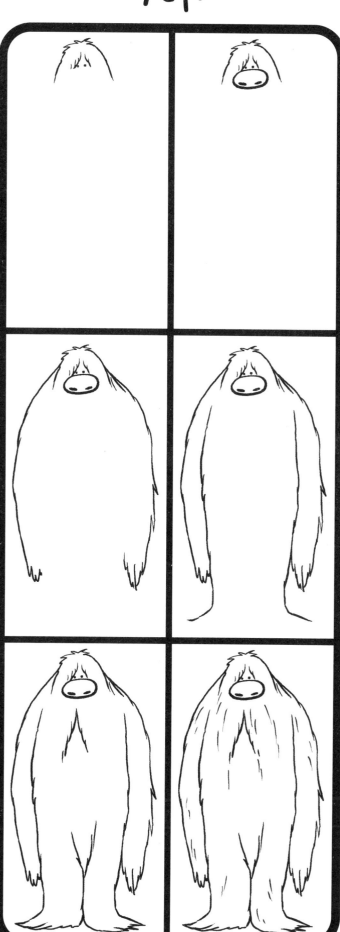

Knight

Dwarf

Witch

Elf King

Phoenix

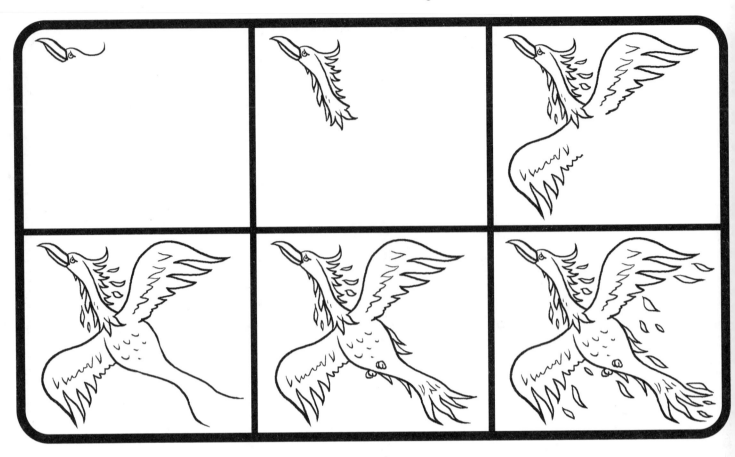

Gremlin

Mermaid

Dragon

Pixie   Zombie

Fairy Queen

Tree Man

Leprechaun

Swamp ogre

Alien

Nymph

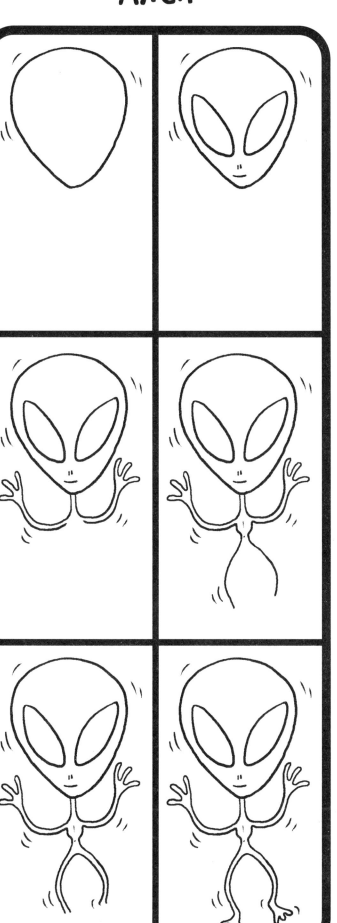

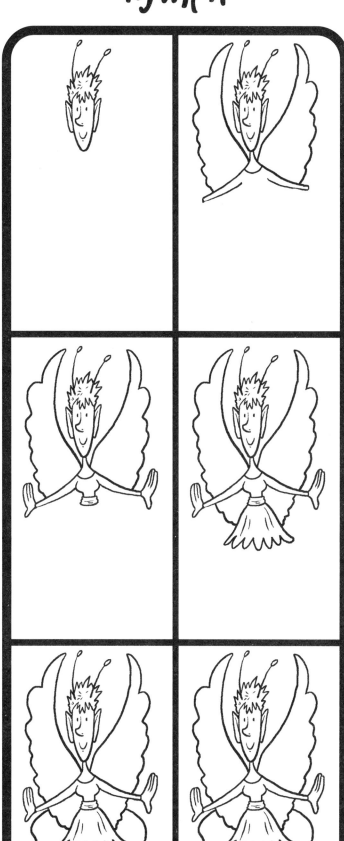

Pegasus

flot Smudger

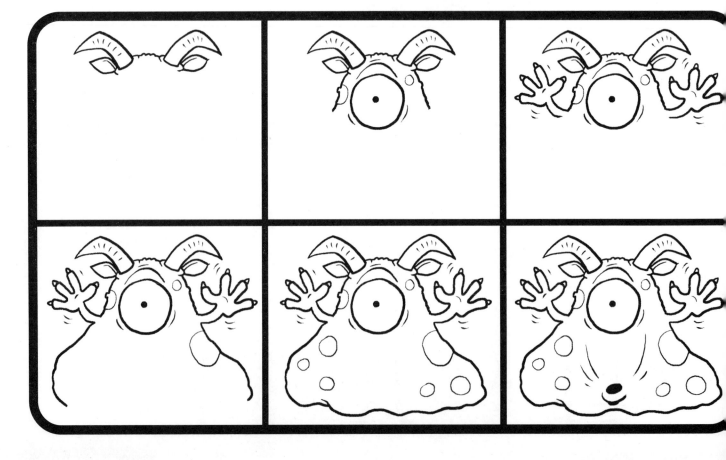

Two-headed Dog

Giant Octopus

Grim Reaper

Prince charming

Jack Frost   # Sorceress

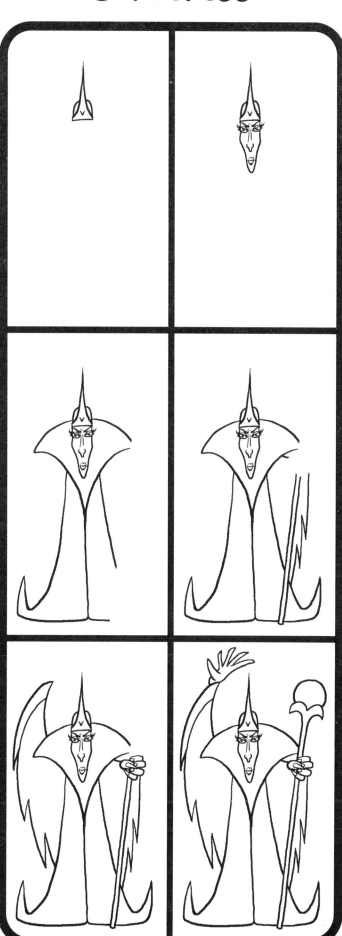

fraggle Snap flower fairy

Gnome

Big Bad Wolf

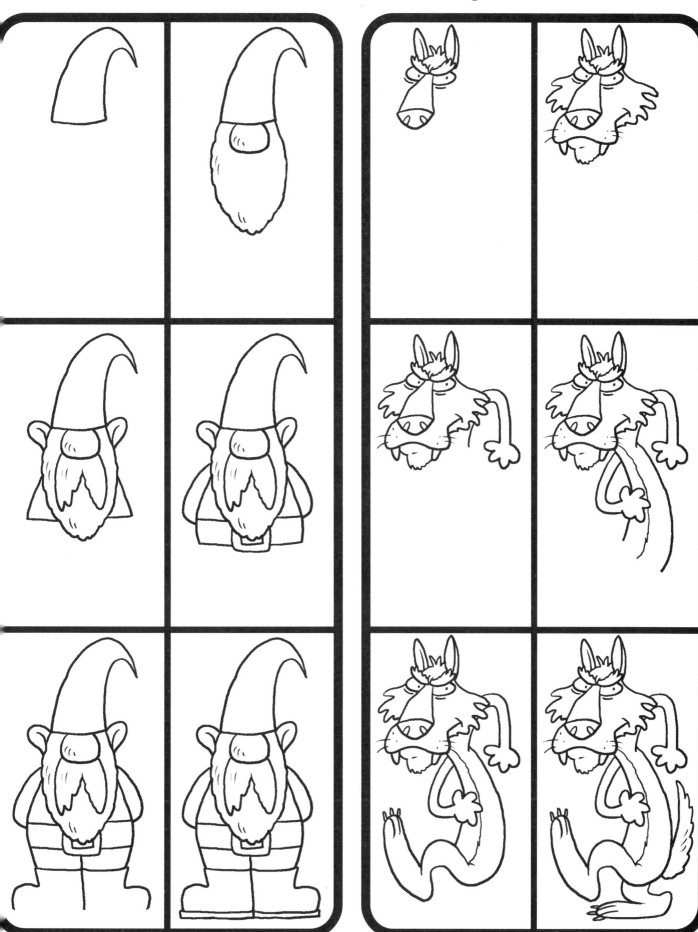

Snotter

Centaur

Thunder Bird

Three-headed ogre

Cave Troll   # Dwarf Lady

Elf Queen

Barbarian

Unicorn

King Poseidon

Lesser-spotted Snotter

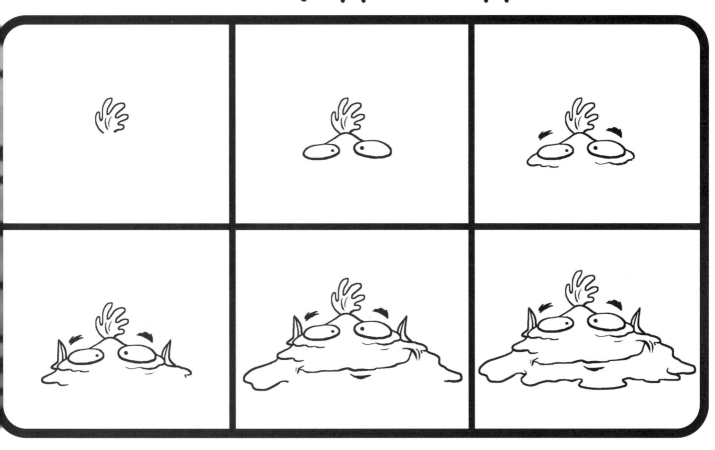

Giant Worm

Hobgoblin

Tree Lady

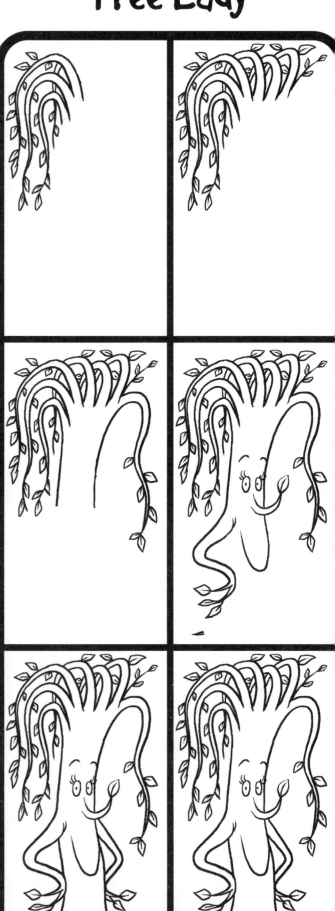

Sorcerer

Big Foot

Wood Troll

Bogeyman

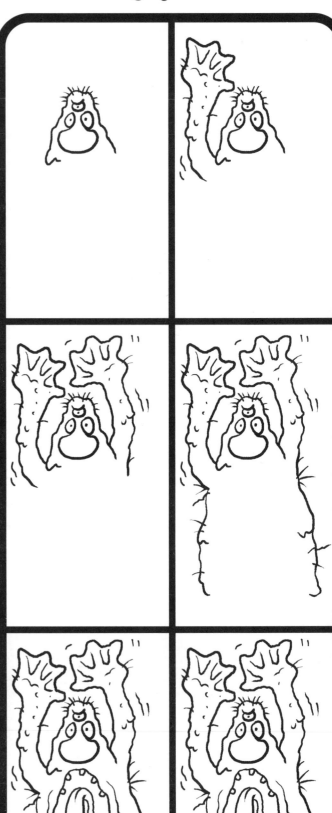

corn fairy

cyclops

Mug Flump

Will'o'Wisp

Sphinx

Griffin

Lizard Man

Sea Troll

White Witch

Nessie

Fairy King

Unifaun

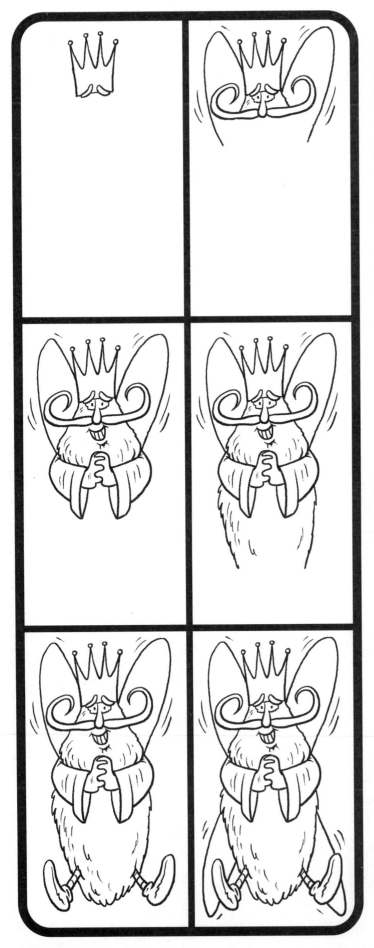

Medusa

Princess

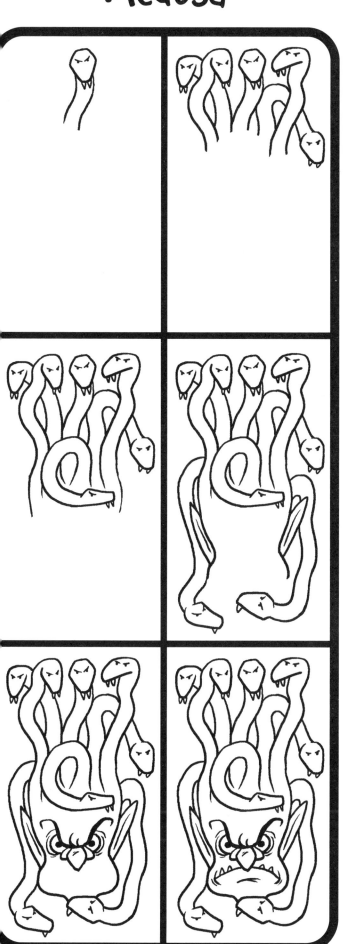

Harpie

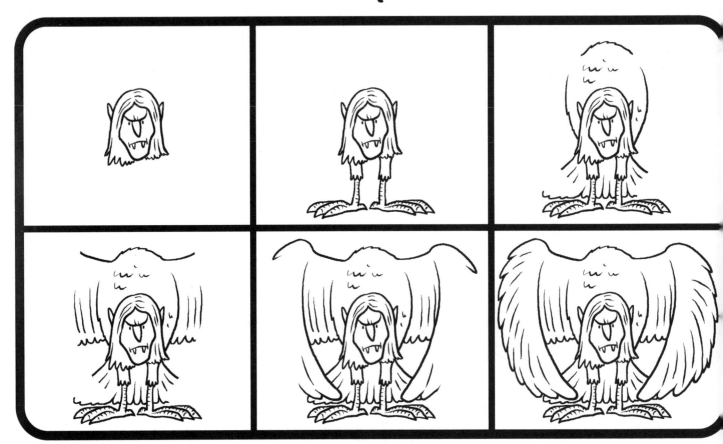

Mushroom Man

Snicker Toad

Giant Spider

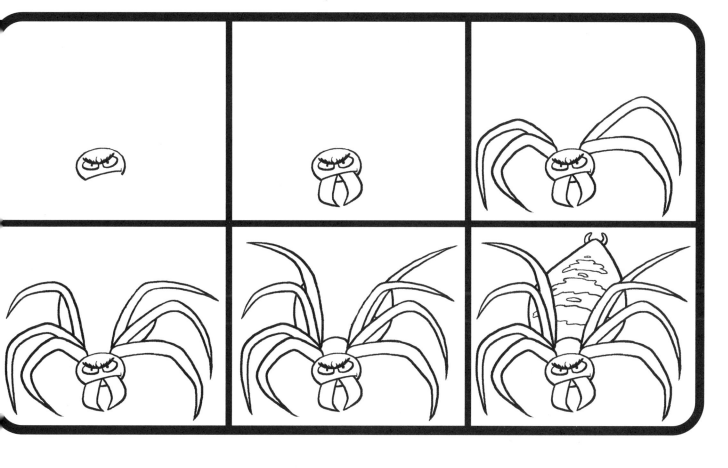

Warlock

Mountain Troll

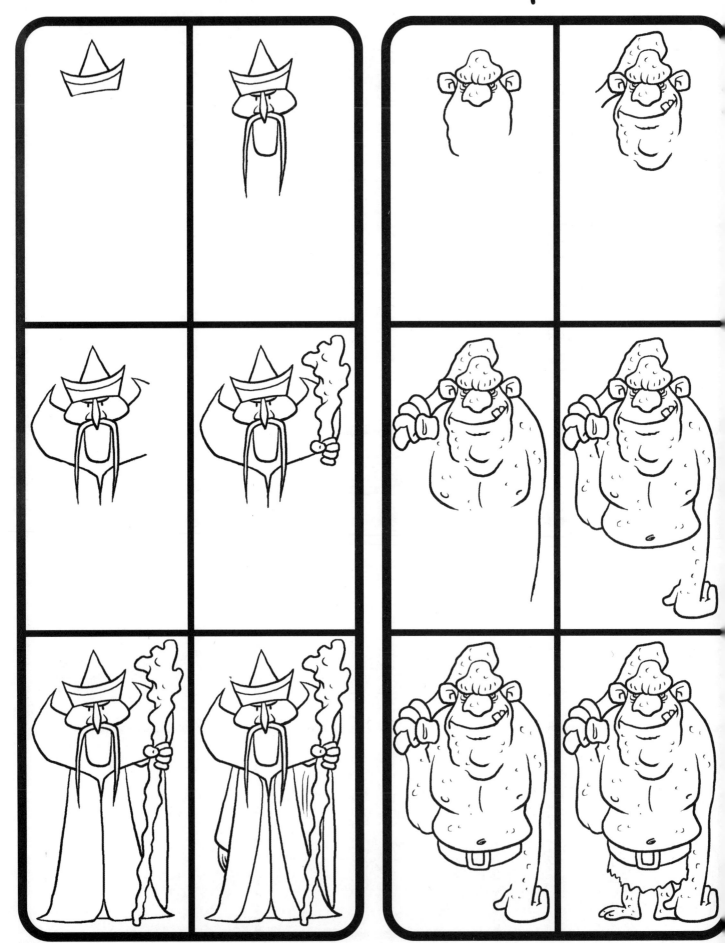

Sandman

Wood Elf

Jabberwocky

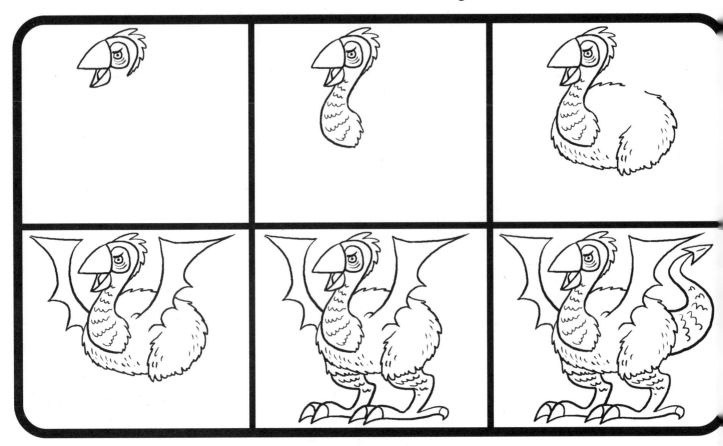

Goat Sucker

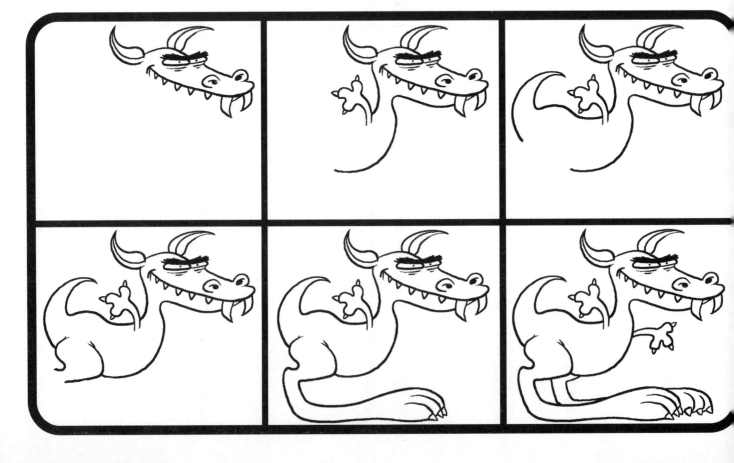

Giant crab

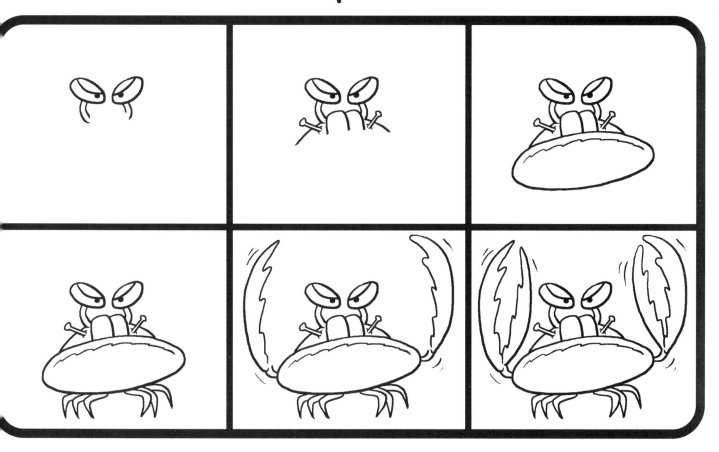

Sprite

Spring-heeled Jack

Siren

Dwarf Lord

Wood Goblin

Gargoyle

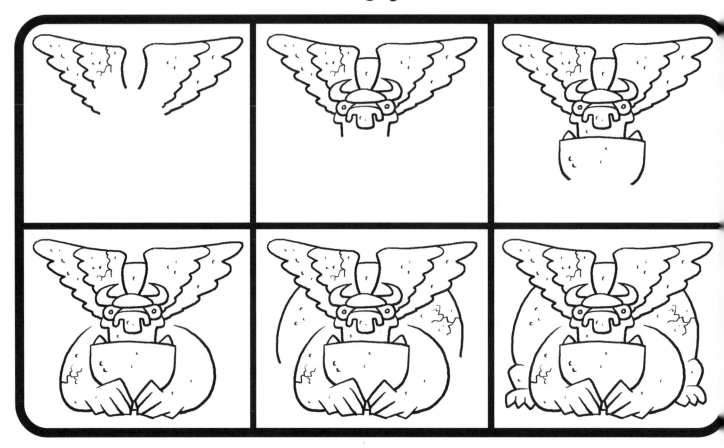

Kraken

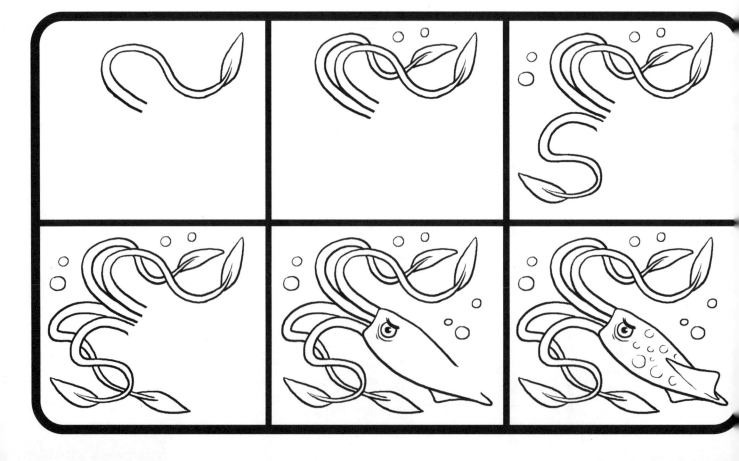

Hippogriff

Bogie

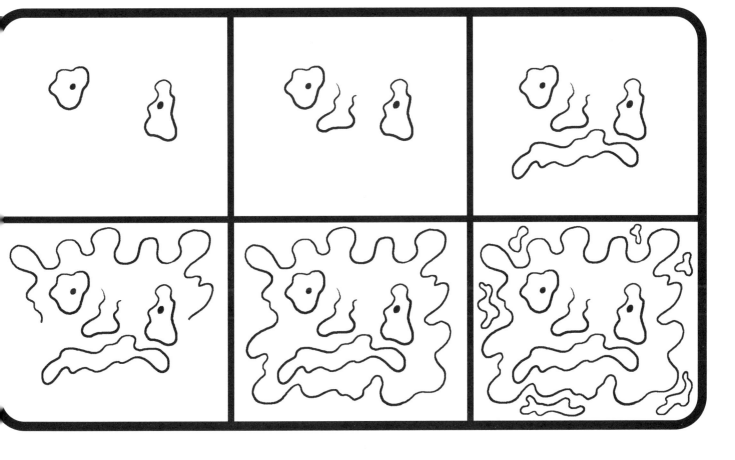

Jub Jub Bird

Cave Goblin

Limey Slop

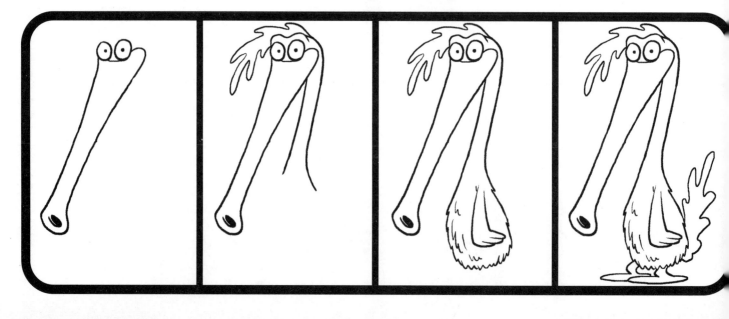

Borogrove

Shape Changer

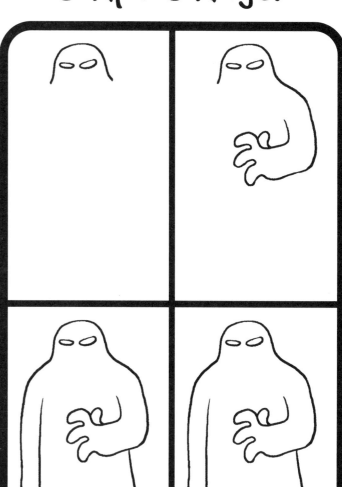

Water Nymph

Snarcrack

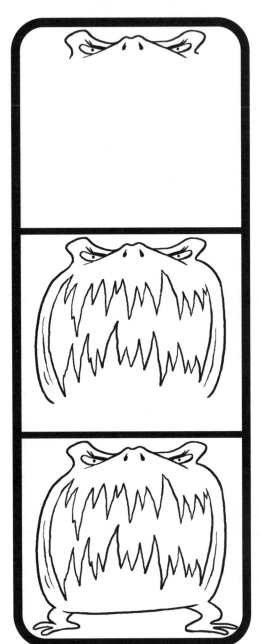

Earth Titan

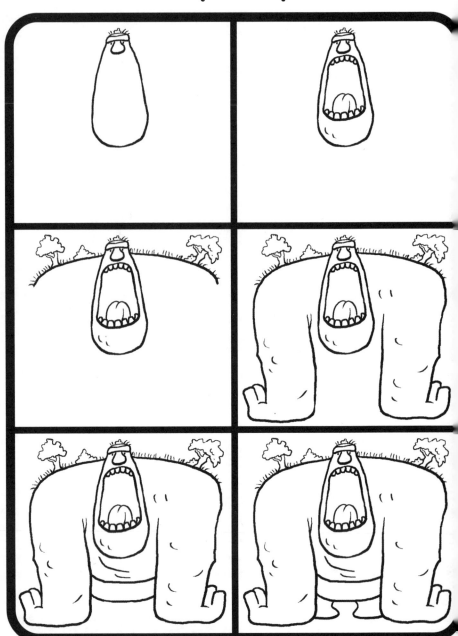

Bander Snatch

Two-headed Snake

Galumph

Hades

Tum Tum

Slithy Tove

Fire Titan

Snakehead

Super Sleuth

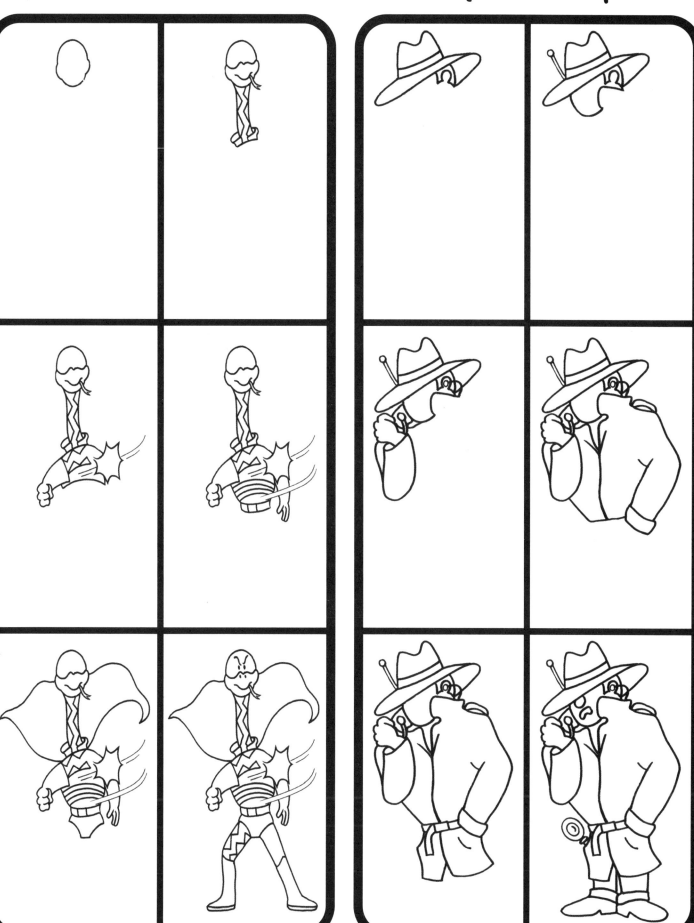

Star Pilot

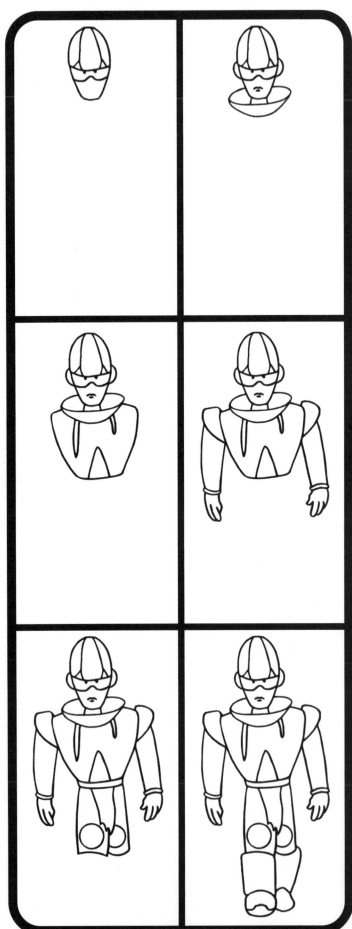

Super Bug

Super Gloo   Princess Mighty

Super Lady   Jaws

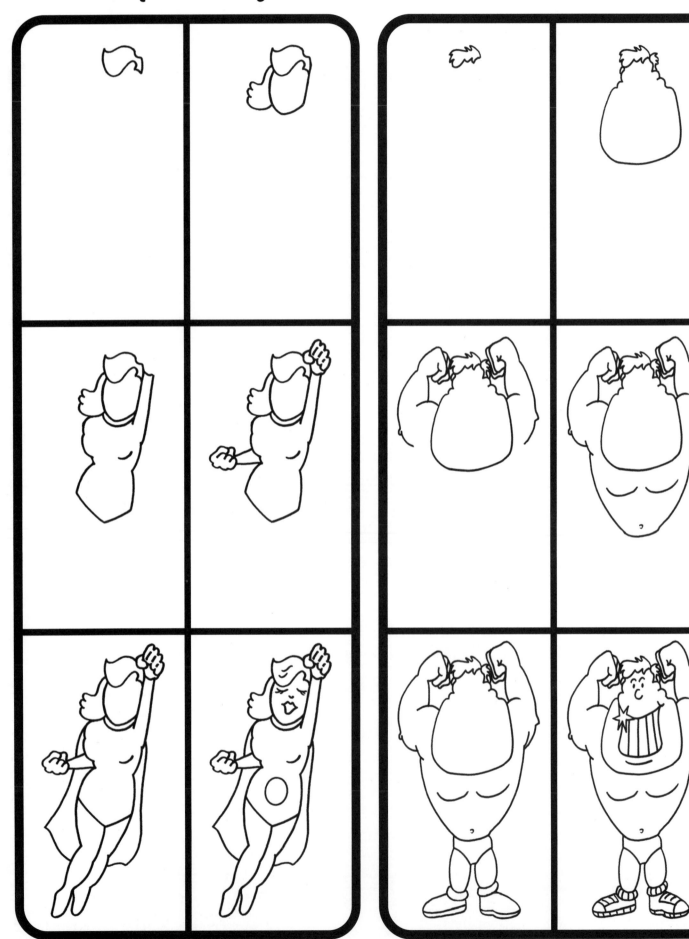

Super Thor   # Super caveman

Blade Warrior   # Celtic Warrior

Super Mum   # Jungle Man

Robin Hood

Dragon Queen

Sir-Lance-A-Lot

Hannibal

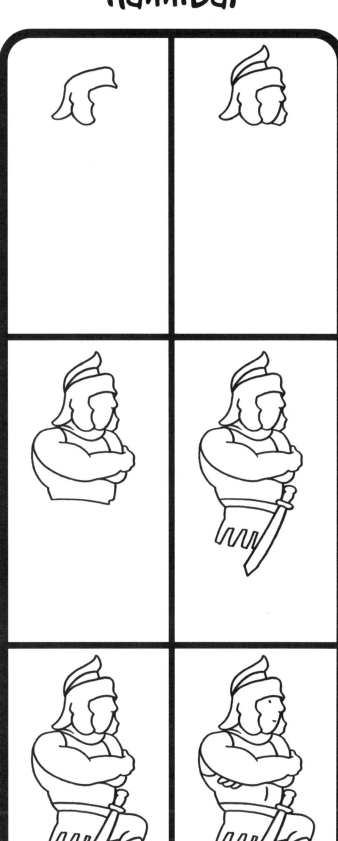

Sir-Lance-A-Lot

Super Duck

Hammer Head

Super Moose

Volgan

Buffalo Bill

Galactica

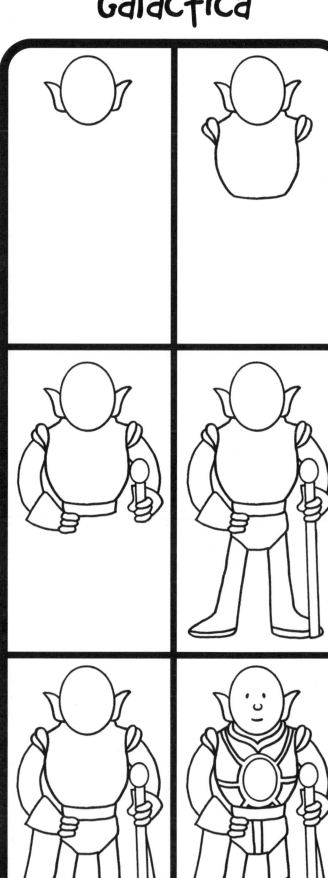

Super oil

Rope Breaker

 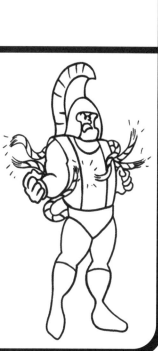

The Bat

Globe Man

Space Robot

Space Baroness

Space Warrior   Sonic Hero

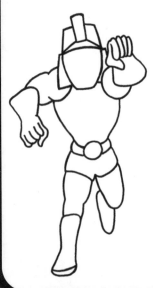

Mechanic Man

Demon Fighter

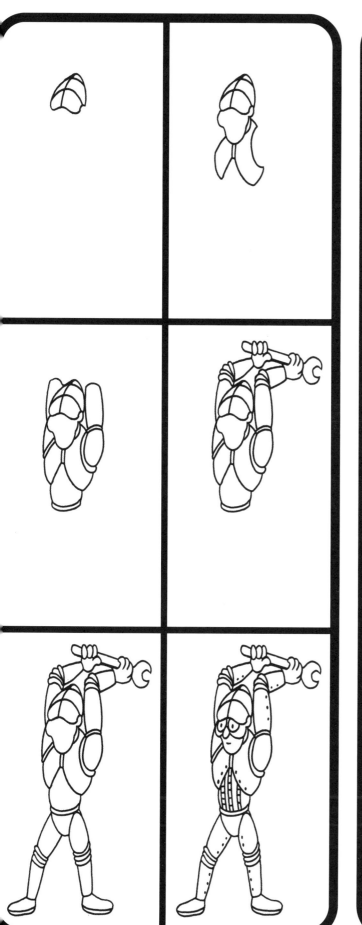

Demon Slayer

Lightning Diver

UDDz

Captain Galactic

Ninja

Axeman

The Archer

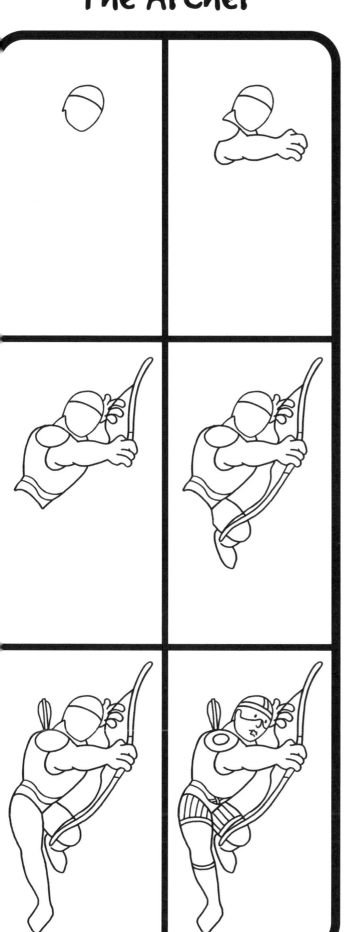

Lightning

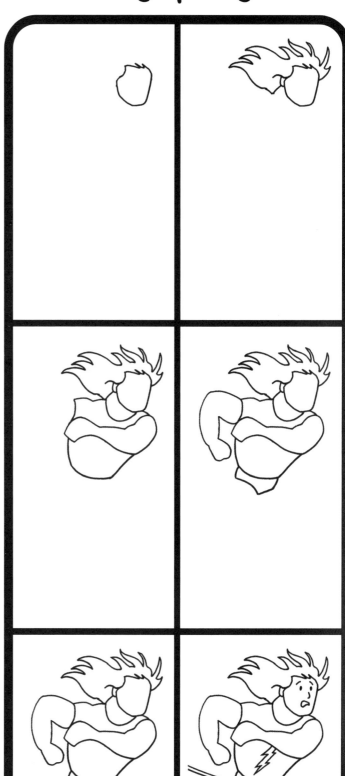

Sky Boxer   Venus Amazon

Star Warden   Spartacus

Star Hunter   Space Shield

Kajo

Zulu

Robot Warrior

Frogman

Space Sniper

Prince Sword

Karate King

Sky Diver

Super Saver

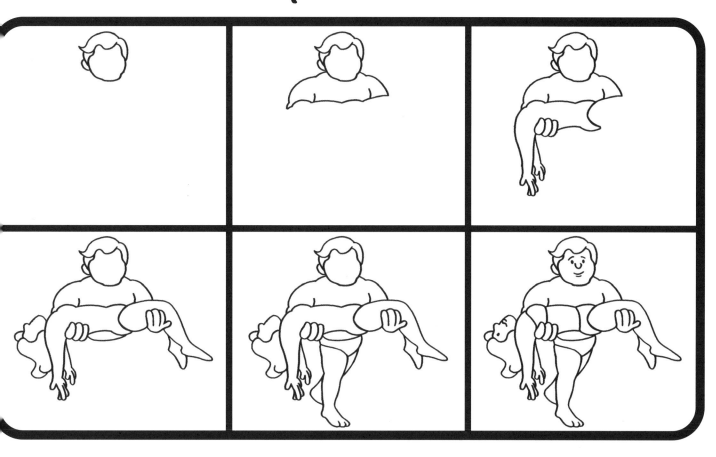

Samurai

Queen Boudicca

Aztec

Super Star

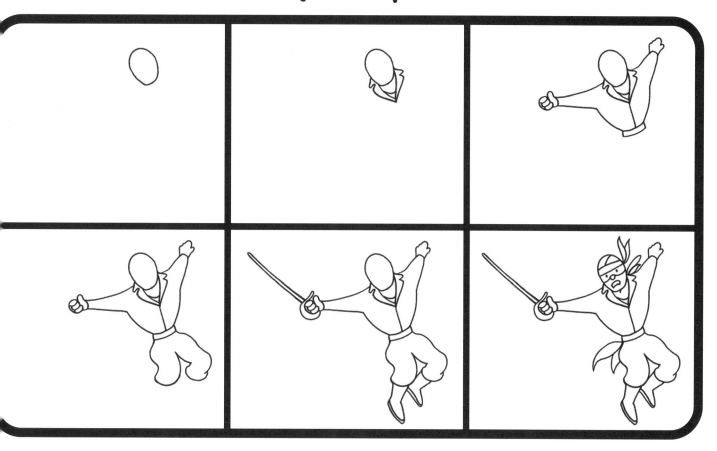

Sky Leaper

Swash Buccaneer

Space Skater

Lizardus

Surf Boarder

Super Egor

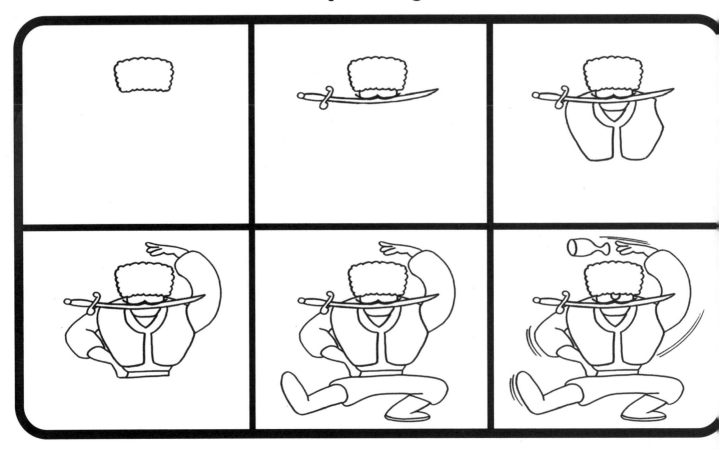

Skater

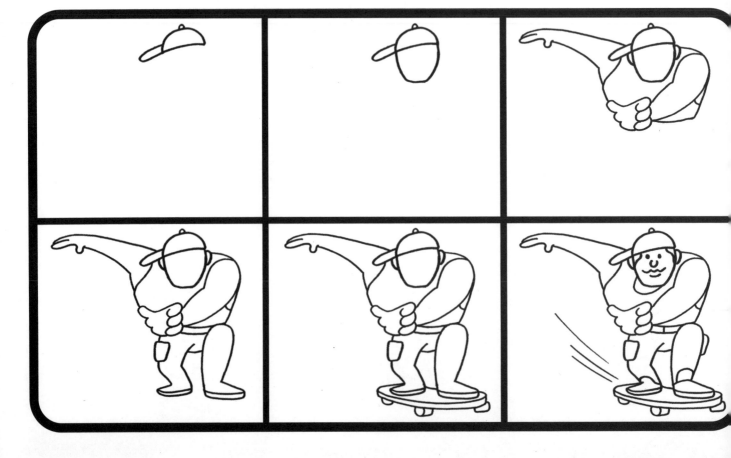

Space Queen

Super Charger

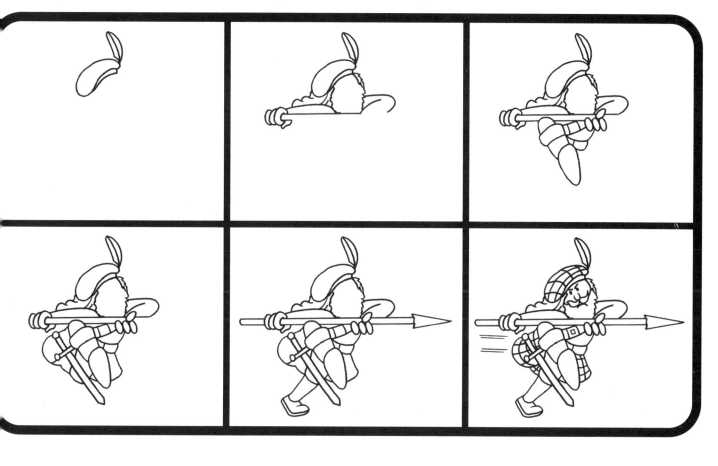

G.I.

Markovian Lancer

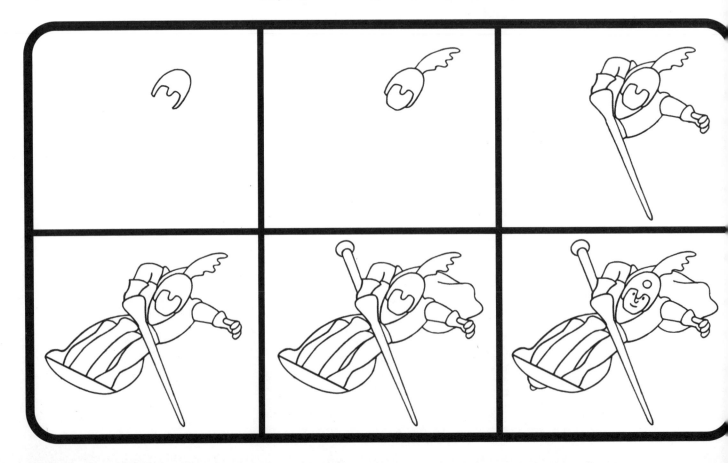

Greek Hero

Sky Scraper

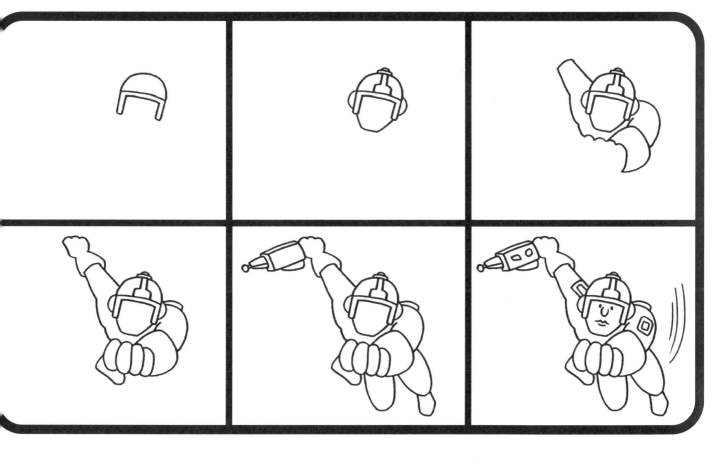

Robo

Kango Kicker

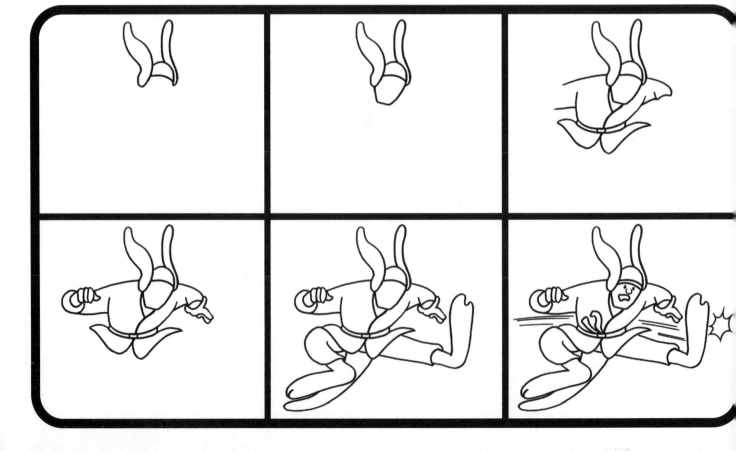

Star Chaser

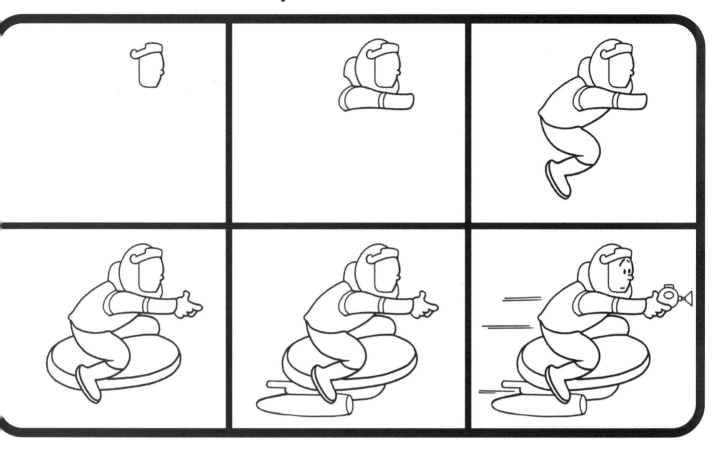

Rocky Hunter

Super Power

Android

Super Silly-us

Kongo

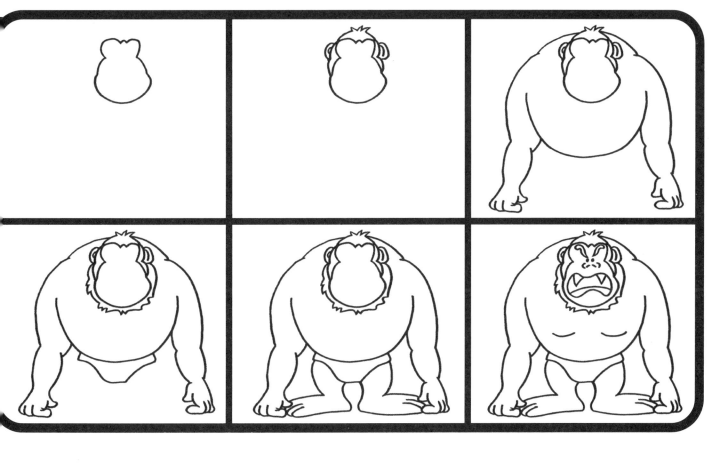

Star Skater

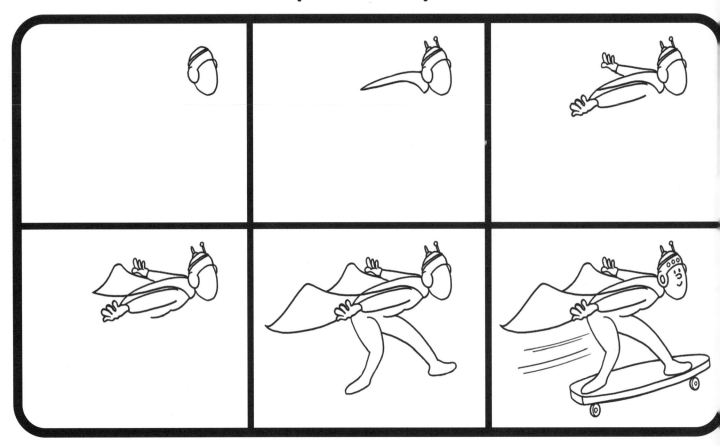

Arachnia

Layzar

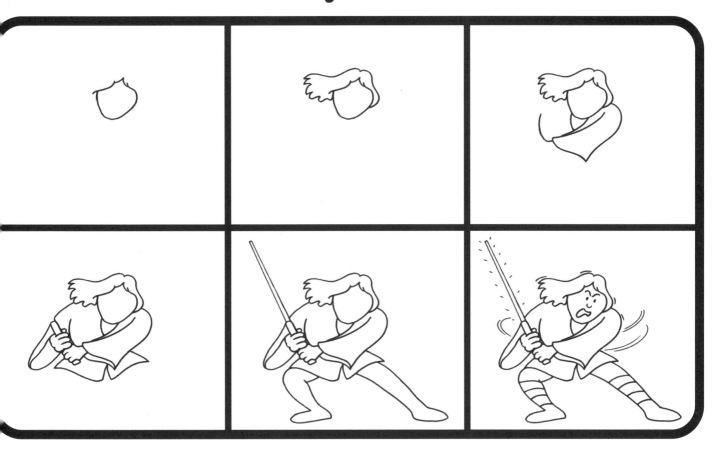

Super Swooper

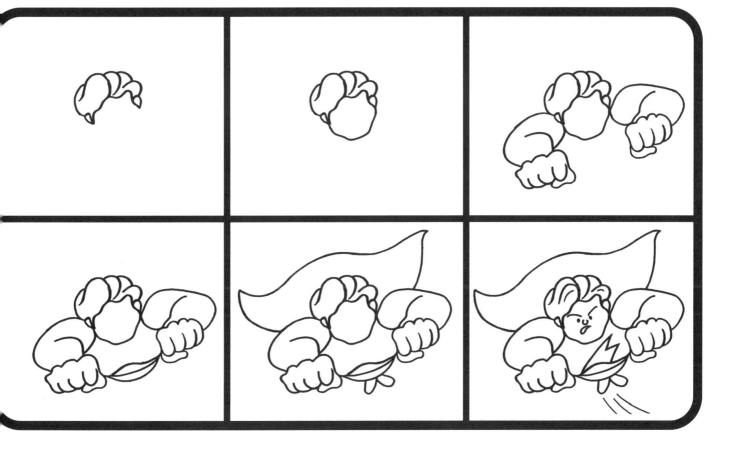

Super Nan

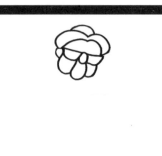

Barbarus

Super Flyer

Space Lancer

Super Spy

Goliath

Sitting Bull

Super Strongman

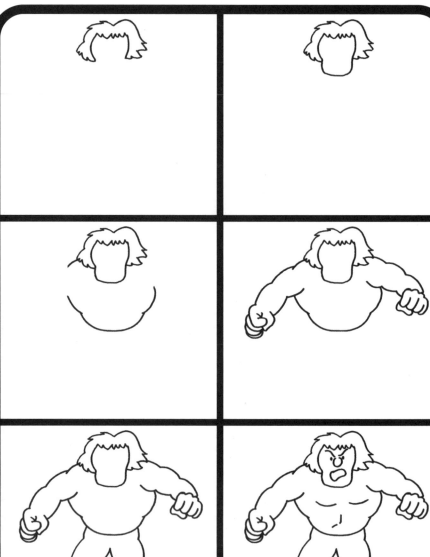

Space Saver

Iron Man

Super Boy

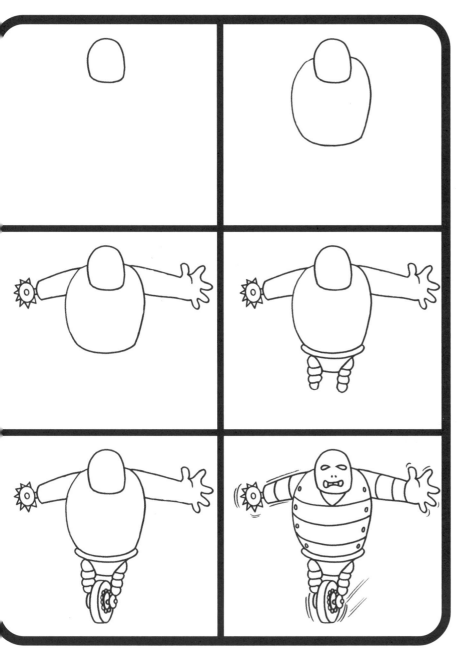
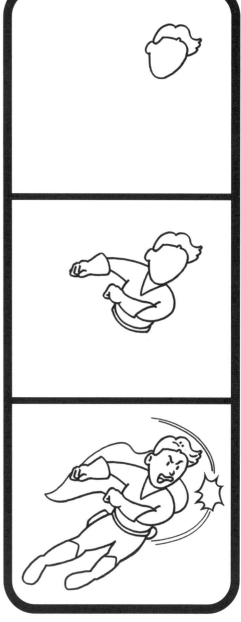

Super Woof

Super Bunny

Big Beard

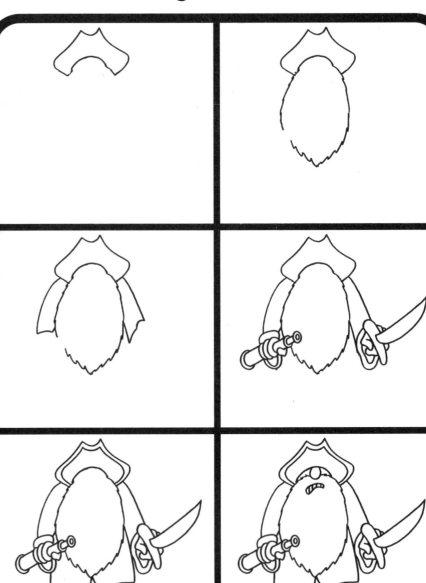

Mighty Mog